Bolstering Vocabulary with Teacher Talk in the Classroom

This practical guide introduces "Teacher Talk," an easy-to-use tool for teachers to help improve elementary students' vocabulary. When students are exposed to extensive vocabularies, they are better prepared to build their receptive and productive language and succeed academically. Through many inviting examples and real-world guidance, Rowe and Haase explain how to be reflective and intentional about the language you use and how to use elevated or substitutionary language to model different registers of speech for elementary students.

The various "Teacher Talk" strategies in this book cover key topics, including disciplinary vocabulary, modelling academic discourse, addressing state and national standards, and meeting individual student needs across grades K–6. With many charts, activities, and tools that are ready for use, this book equips teachers with many methods for bolstering students' academic language in the classroom and beyond.

Kristen Haase is an elementary ESL teacher in Pennsylvania, where she also serves as the ELD team leader and is a member of the school's leadership team.

Carmen Shahadi Rowe is an ESL instructional coach for an urban school district in Pennsylvania. She has served as a Spanish and K–12 ESL teacher and administrator at the district level and is the founder of Accelerating Language, LLC.

Other Eye on Education Books Available from Routledge

(www.routledge.com/eyeoneducation)

School-wide Systems for Multilingual Learner Success
A Roadmap for Leaders
Lisa Auslander and Joanna Yip

Vocabulary Strategies that Work, Second Edition
Do This – Not That!
Lori Wilfong

Engaging the Families of Els and Immigrants
Ideas, Resources, and Activities
Renee Rubin, Michelle H. Abrego, and John A. Sutterby

Remote Teaching and Learning in the Middle and High ELA Classroom
Instructional Strategies and Best Practices
Sean Ruday and Jennifer Cassidy

Remote Teaching and Learning in the Elementary ELA Classroom
Instructional Strategies and Best Practices
Sean Ruday and Jennifer Cassidy

The Middle School Grammar Toolkit, Second Edition
Using Mentor Texts to Teach Standards-Based Language and Grammar in Grades 6–8
Sean Ruday

The Elementary School Grammar Toolkit, Second Edition
Using Mentor Texts to Teach Standards-Based Language and Grammar in Grades 3–5
Sean Ruday

Student-Centered Literacy Assessment in the 6–12 Classroom
An Asset-Based Approach
Sean Ruday and Katie Caprino

Inquiry-Based Literature Instruction in the 6–12 Classroom:
A Hands-on Guide for Deeper Learning
Sean Ruday and Katie Caprino

The First-Year English Teacher's Guidebook
Strategies for Success
Sean Ruday

Bolstering Vocabulary with Teacher Talk in the Classroom

Strategic Modeling to Elevate Students' Language

Kristen Haase and Carmen Shahadi Rowe

Routledge
Taylor & Francis Group
NEW YORK AND LONDON

Designed cover image: Kristen Haase and Carmen Shahadi Rowe

First published 2023
by Routledge
605 Third Avenue, New York, NY 10158

and by Routledge
4 Park Square, Milton Park, Abingdon, Oxon, OX14 4RN

Routledge is an imprint of the Taylor & Francis Group, an informa business

Library of Congress Cataloging-in-Publication Data
A catalog record for this book has been requested

ISBN: 978-1-032-28205-3 (hbk)
ISBN: 978-1-032-26216-1 (pbk)
ISBN: 978-1-003-29571-6 (ebk)

DOI: 10.4324/9781003295716

Typeset in Palatino
by Apex CoVantage, LLC

This book is dedicated to my remarkable husband, Rick, a musician by trade, a teacher and shepherd at heart. ~Carmen

To Justin, my rock, and Evan, my purpose. ~Kristen

Contents

Meet the Authors

Kristen Haase, M.A., is an elementary English as a second language teacher at a medium-sized urban school district in Pennsylvania. Currently, she is on the equity team for her district and serves on the leadership team at her school. She is a Fellow for Teach Plus PA and will serve as a Senior Policy Fellow in next year's cohort. As a member of Teach Plus, she has met with legislators across the state of Pennsylvania, advocating for meaningful education policy for her students and her colleagues. In March of 2022, her op-ed on the teacher shortage crisis was published. She is a former adjunct professor for Millersville University and Harrisburg Area Community College. She earned her bachelor's degree in Spanish education from the University of Delaware and her master's degree in teaching English as a second language from West Chester University. She lives with her husband and son.

Carmen Shahadi Rowe, Ed.D., is currently an ESL coach for an urban district in Pennsylvania. She has served as a Spanish and ESL (K–12) teacher and an administrator at the district level. She is the founder of Accelerating Language, LLC. The company's mission is to equip educators with skills and strategies for developing robust academic language for all students. She currently does consulting work for public schools, education service agencies, the Pennsylvania Department of Education, and the Center for Schools and Communities. She earned her master's in TESOL from Eastern Mennonite University and her doctorate in educational leadership from Immaculata University. Her dissertation focused on the implementation of co-teaching with English language learners. In addition to her experience in public education, she teaches graduate courses for Millersville University, Eastern Mennonite University, and the Chester County Intermediate Unit. She is actively involved in community service and advocacy and frequently provides professional development on topics related to education throughout the State of Pennsylvania. She has published articles and contributed a chapter to the book titled *Composing Storylines of Possibilities: Immigrant and Refugee Families Navigating School*. She has broadened her horizons through studying abroad and traveling extensively, but her best education has come from being a first-generation American born to immigrant and refugee parents *and* parenting eight amazing and talented children with her amazing and talented husband, Rick.

Acknowledgments

To the individuals at Routledge Publishing who made this book possible, we are forever grateful: Lauren Davis, our first contact at Routledge, who connected us to all the right people; Editorial Assistants Emily Dombrovskaya and Katherine Tsamparlis, who answered our questions about the submission process; and to Karen Adler, who delivered the news that the editorial board at Routledge unanimously approved our proposal and helped lead us to publication. We also grateful for Ramachandran Vijayaraghavan our project manager and Kim Husband our copyeditor.

We are indebted to the invaluable contributions made by our fellow English as a second language colleagues, Yara Graupera and Jeanne Oakes. Yara's help as a researcher helped moved our work along in strategic ways. Both Yara and Jeanne were instrumental in conducting action research in the field and provided useful feedback to the authors. As mentioned in Chapter 5, together, they initiated a grassroots schoolwide culture of elevated language and shared numerous anecdotes on the process.

The authors are grateful for the mentors in their lives. The authors would like to thank their dear friend and former colleague Vicki Legath for sharing her experiences about her granddaughter. She is Kristen's former mentor and confidant. We are indebted to our respected friend, university professor, and author Persida Himmele. She provided guidance on numerous occasions that helped set us on the right path. We are grateful for her valuable counsel. Carmen is grateful for Persida's mentorship in her life. A huge thank-you to master ESL teacher Janet Purcell for allowing us to highlight some of her original strategies. Carmen is thankful for her friendship and mentoring. We would like to thank our many friends and colleagues who contributed to this book, some of whom shared their original thoughts and ideas and others who were willing to explore new strategies and provide feedback.

A project of this magnitude would not have been possible without the expertise of teachers in the field. The authors would like to recognize veteran teacher Lenore Charnock, who is always willing to try new ideas and reflect on her practice regularly; Ben Jackson, who is a creative literary genius and master of figurative language; master teacher Allyson Plasterer, who has taught the authors so much about the importance of skills and strategies; Matt Pavelko, who brings academic vocabulary to his music classroom and his daily conversations with students; Amanda Aikens, former elementary teacher and current instructional coach, who provided feedback; and English as a second language teacher Marco Ortiz, who brings a wealth of experience and creativity to the field of language teaching.

The authors would also like to thank a band of teachers who supported the grassroots movement started by Yara and Jeannie. Many thanks go to veteran teachers Barb Heister and Vicki Stutz, who provided valuable insights and feedback during our times of reflection, and to intermediate teacher Leah Flick, who was willing to try new strategies. In addition, the authors would like to acknowledge a group of pre-K coaches who work with younger learners to bolster teacher talk. Many thanks to Kelly Adams for adapting the strategies for her students and to veteran coaches Trudy Eby and Barb Schimd, who shared their invaluable expertise and insight into the pragmatics of language learning in regard to younger learners.

The authors would also like to extend a special thanks to Dr. Damaris Rau for always supporting us as educators and giving us the green light to begin our journey as published co-authors. Thanks to Ryan Stralo, Karen Wynn, and Shannon Smith, who helped secure our Memorandum of Understanding with the district and answered our questions all along the way. The authors are deeply grateful for the contributions of former seasoned principals Wanda Ramirez Suarez and Camille Hopkins, who generously shared their invaluable expertise on building a schoolwide culture of elevated language. Much thanks is extended to principal Rachel Esh for believing in the importance of elevated language enough to invite the authors to provide a year-long series of professional development around elevated language and the principle of substitutionary language.

The authors would like to extend a special thanks to Kristen's father for his practical business advice.

Kristen would like to acknowledge members of her family. She is grateful for her husband, Justin Haase, for his never-ending support, sacrifice, and understanding and to her son, Evan Haase, who is her inspiration and her muse. She thanks her parents, Richard and Nancy Posey, for being a part of the editing and research-gathering processes. She owes much gratitude to her aunt and master teacher, Judy Lewandowski, for reading through the first drafts of the book and providing professional advice. Carmen expresses gratitude to her husband, Rick Rowe, for his sacrifice, encouragement, and inspiration for and modeling of ideas for much of the chapter on *Engaging Caregivers*. She thanks her children, Benjamin, Josh, Sarah, Zech, Abby, Peter, Danny, and Gabe: our remarkable eight children who were her first students. She acknowledges her amazing daughters and daughters-in-law, who model elevated language to their children. Thanks also to Izzy, Emma, Jack, Olivia, Gracie, Tommy, Hudson, Kate, Canaan, Evie, and Mara, our 11 grandchildren extraordinaire. Finally, gratitude to Casper and Elsie Shade, her parents and first teachers. Thank you to all our friends and family, too numerous to mention, who supported us throughout this journey.

Another group to be thanked is our students over the years. They have inspired us to reflect on our practice and to become better teachers. Their perseverance to learn English served as our inspiration to write this book. There are too many to thank personally, but we hope they have learned as much from us as we have learned from them.

Preface

With a combined total of 35 years in education spanning K–12 to higher education, Kristen and Carmen traveled their unique roads in public education. Eventually, their paths would cross in an urban district, both members of the same English language development department. Each teacher had experienced great success with increasing students' vocabularies, as well as discourse, in their own classrooms. They soon would discover that not only did they share a passion for providing equity to their students through the purposeful modeling of elevated language, but they also used the same approach in raising their own children.

They became increasingly mindful of their own "teacher talk" and deliberately and systematically elevated their own language for their children and students. Through subsequent conversations with each other, they proposed the impact that a common school culture could have if every teacher were to model elevated language in his or her speech throughout the school day. This led to a series of ongoing and sustained professional-development trainings throughout the school year.

They led teachers through a three-part series on teacher talk. During the first session, they introduced the principle of substitutionary language and the importance of using it in every interaction with students. The second focused on using substitutionary language during routines and instruction. Lastly, they discussed the importance of teacher talk outside of the classroom: in the halls, in the cafeteria, and during impromptu conversations. From these professional-development sessions and ongoing, evolving conversations, the idea of the book was born.

Introduction

We understand that there is much competing for your time: lesson planning, addressing the standards, classroom management, and meeting the individual needs of your students. The list could go on. Teacher Talk is not a program but rather a tool for teachers to use that will bolster students' vocabularies across all content areas. Through conscious reflection and becoming more aware of every word in our own speech, we can become the powerful role models that our students deserve and so desperately need. Each chapter provides background knowledge on the topic and reflection activities as well as strategies for bolstering your teacher talk through strategic modeling.

Chapter Overview

In Chapter 1, the reader will be presented with a strong rationale for why all teachers at every grade level and every subject area should be implementing elevated language throughout the instructional day as well as outside the instructional day. The chapter gives the readers an opportunity to reflect on their current use of elevated language throughout their day.

In Chapter 2, readers will gain an understanding of the principle of substitutionary language, substituting more common words for more nuanced and academic terms once certain conditions are met. The reader will understand how the principle can bolster all students' language through strategic modeling. Upon completion of the chapter, readers will have an understanding of what substitutionary language is and is not.

DOI: 10.4324/9781003295716-1

In Chapter 3, the reader will explore the research that supports bolstering vocabulary with teacher talk. Readers will learn about the importance of oral language in regard to the early childhood classroom, the literacy classroom, and the English language learner classroom.

In Chapter 4, the reader will investigate practical strategies and tools in order to bolster their teacher talk. The strategies, all of which have been used successfully in the classroom, offer ideas for teachers of all different levels and subject areas. Quotes and anecdotes from new and veteran teachers alike provide the rationale and the buy-in for shifting the reader's mindset to use elevated language in each and every interaction with their students.

In Chapter 5, the reader will understand the importance of creating a schoolwide culture in which all stakeholders within a school building realize the importance of using elevated language with their students throughout the school day. A strong argument will be made from school administrators and teachers on how to go about collecting meaningful data as well as creating and maintaining this culture.

In Chapter 6, the reader will become familiar with ways in which to engage parents in the work of developing robust vocabularies with their children using the principle of substitutionary language. By seizing opportunities that occur through common daily routines and household activities, parents can use the strategies introduced in this chapter to bolster their children's vocabularies in unique and powerful ways.

While the primary audience for this book is K–6 teachers, educators of other levels can find relevance in the topic. The first three chapters set the rationale for bolstering vocabulary with teacher talk. These chapters set the stage and get the readers thinking of the importance of their words. After the compelling argument for teacher talk is made, Chapter 4 dives into the application of modeling teacher talk through a myriad of strategies. Many of these strategies can be adapted to any level. Those highlighted below would have great relevance for older elementary and secondary students:

- Strategy #1, Ridding Ourselves of Informal Language, provides tips for eliminating informal contractions and vague language from your teacher talk.
- Strategy #2, Using Substitutionary Language While Giving Directions, gives numerous suggestions for replacing common language associated with giving directions with more elevated language. This strategy is especially applicable because teachers at any grade level give directives multiple times throughout the school day.
- Strategy #4, Using Content Vocabulary Across the Curriculum, provides ideas on how teachers can use content-area vocabulary

across the curriculum. This strategy allows teachers to reflect on how they could use academic vocabulary from other subject areas in their specific content instruction.

- Strategy #10, Modeling Elevated Language at the Discourse Level, offers ways for teachers to strategically model academic discourse through their teacher talk. Secondary teachers often have the opportunity to connect with students by engaging them in conversations centering around their interests both inside and outside of the classroom.
- Strategy #11, Modeling Discourse to Address the Common Core Standards, provides a rationale for modeling your teacher talk so that it mirrors the standards by infusing the language and the structure of academic discourse in teacher–student interactions. This strategy presents the reader with ways to model and develop discourse around the functions of language such as explaining, arguing, and persuading.

Tips for Reading this Book

Before you get started, here are some helpful tips:

- Take your time reading the book. Do not read it the whole way through before putting some of the ideas into practice.
- After you try some of the ideas, reflect on them. Was it a challenge to use substitutionary language, or did it come naturally? How did your students respond? What could you do differently?
- Take notes as you read. Use the book as a workbook. Process new ideas and reflect on your own practice.
- Consider allowing a trusted colleague to observe your practice as you develop elevated language.
- Complete as a book study with colleagues. By teaming up with a colleague, you can hold each other accountable, brainstorm ideas together, and observe each other's practice in action.

Pre-Reading Assignment

STOP

Before you read on, please complete the following task. Collect speaking samples of yourself that include the following:

- Giving directions in the classroom
- Giving directions outside of the classroom

- Answering a student's question
- Greeting students
- Engaging in morning routines

***The more information you can collect, the more meaningful the reflection activities will be.

Dos and Don'ts for Collecting Speaking Samples

Do:	Don't:
Complete this activity, because it will provide an opportunity to reflect on your current practice.	Skip this request, as several activities are based on these recordings.
Take advantage of an opportunity to hear yourself objectively and notice things you will miss when listening in the moment.	Believe you are already aware of what you sound like when talking; you may be in for a surprise.
Use spontaneous language to record.	Rehearse your speech or read directly from a script or a text.

1

Prepared for Life

Why Is Teacher Talk Important?

Now more than ever, we realize the importance of providing an education that leads to equity and equality for all students. What is one way to do this? By empowering students: this is our job as teachers. One of the greatest ways to empower our students is to expose them to high level vocabulary and academic discourse in order to expand their vocabularies and enhance their language skills. If you are having trouble envisioning this, we introduce you to Moira Rose of *Schitt's Creek*. In this short video clip, we witness Moira, of *Schitt's Creek*, converse with others using the most robust of vocabularies, including words such as "pettifogging," "bedeviled," "chanteuse," and "confabulate." While she leaves some asking, "What are you saying?" she holds our interest while entertaining us and putting a smile on our face.

Moira Rose in Action

DOI: 10.4324/9781003295716-2

Having an expanded vocabulary is necessary to succeed in academic settings, job interviews, networking, and business. When students possess extensive vocabularies and use a variety of sentence structures in their productive language, they feel not only smart but also confident. This leads to students speaking and writing with greater ease as they know and understand the precise vocabulary to use in each and every situation. Building extensive vocabularies does not happen by accident. It is the result of reflective teachers who weigh each word!

Creating a safe environment in which students are willing to take risks and make mistakes is paramount to learning. While we need to be on our guard in an effort to protect and shield students from unnecessary failure and embarrassment, we do not want to stifle them. Verplaetse (1998) coined the phrase the "Benevolent Conspiracy" to warn educators to be on their guard against inadvertently lowering expectations by withholding open-ended and higher-order-thinking questions from English learners. In a similar vein, we need to be sure to use elevated language with all students and avoid sheltering those we deem "not ready" or "unable to comprehend" what we call elevated language. Students who lack robust and sophisticated vocabularies need teachers who are committed to modeling elevated language for them. In this way, students have an opportunity to build their receptive listening and reading vocabularies and will eventually risk "trying on" the language in their productive vocabularies.

College and Career Readiness: Tales From the Classroom

Without a solid, proficient command of the English language, our students will not be prepared for either college or careers. As a college instructor for more than 10 years, Dr. Carmen Shahadi Rowe had the pleasure of teaching many talented, reflective, and aspiring teachers. In a required course designed to equip teachers with strategies for teaching English learners, one particular student of hers comes to mind. A former English learner, this student was passionate about the call to become a teacher. He readily and fervently shared during class discussions his struggles as a student and how he desired to help others achieve academically. Therein lay the problem. While his anecdotes were compelling and his language diversity an asset, his use of proper English language was lacking. Carmen approached him early in the course and asked him if she could help him edit his papers. He was very open to the help. Sadly, although he received help from his professors and the writing lab, his lack of command of academic English was too much to overcome.

Not long after, Carmen learned he had switched his major. This student's story is a reminder to us all of the importance of making sure all students are college and career ready. One key aspect of the readiness is empowering them with robust vocabularies.

Oftentimes, individuals view language diversity in one of two ways: as an asset or a deficit. Delpit (2006) challenged educators to choose a perspective from which to view the various languages that exist in our classrooms as assets, whether the differences come from other world languages or those from other dialects. Viewing languages and dialects as part of one's culture and therein as an asset is only the first step in equipping our children for a culturally diverse world.

Delpit (2006) stated,

> We can continue to view diversity as a problem, attempting to force all differences into standardized boxes. Or we can recognize that diversity of thought, language, and worldview in our classrooms cannot only provide an exciting educational setting but can also prepare our children for the richness of living in an increasingly diverse national community.
>
> (pp. 66–67)

In addition to recognizing that diversity of language is an asset both to individuals and to the classroom, we must also point out to students that their own language, or dialect, albeit different from standard English, is every bit as valuable. Language is the means by which we communicate with others. In pointing out the value in possessing more than one language or dialect, students and teachers will begin to see all language as an asset instead of a deficit.

Code-switching (Appel & Muysken, 2005) refers to one's ability to move between two languages or dialects during a single conversation or situation. Code-switching can be taught to students in a way that value is given to both languages or dialects. Instead of choosing between the formal academic English register and other forms and dialects, Emdin (2016) suggested that we teach students to become code-switchers, individuals who are able to navigate between two or more languages, and to value not only the English academic register but also the languages that students bring with them. Emdin emphasized that as students are explicitly taught to code switch, they will gain an appreciation for the value that each language has in unique spaces.

In the world of academics, we most certainly encounter a more formal register or language than we do when interacting socially with our family and friends. Consider the following opening sentence of the Declaration of Independence typically studied as part of a United States social studies curriculum:

High-Level Language

When, **in the course of human events, it becomes necessary for one people to dissolve** the **political bonds which** have connected **them** with **another,** and **to assume, among the powers of the earth, the separate and equal station to which the laws of nature and nature's God entitle them, a decent respect to the opinions of mankind requires** that **they** should **declare** the **causes which impel them to the separation.**

This is not the language we hear in social situations, and according to the experts, it is not being used much in classrooms, either (Filmore & Filmore, 2012). It is, however, the language of textbooks. The vast amount of educational manuals, textbooks, and literature is written in a formal register. To deny students access to formal academic standard English is to deny them opportunity. In addition, to not expose students to a formal register with its unique grammatical forms and functions is to deny them access to a robust education that prepares them for any one of a multitude of careers. Moreover, using a common academic register in school allows us to use precise language to express our thoughts so that all may understand the messages shared, whether orally or in writing.

Although both types of registers, formal and informal, have value, the formal academic register is most often modeled and accessed in classroom or educational settings. For this reason, teachers need not only to explicitly teach this type of language and how it differs from social language and other codes but also to strategically model it in their speech. When students are exposed to multiple repetitions of this elevated language, they will eventually acquire it as part of their own speaking and writing or "productive language." Rowe and Suarez (2019) further emphasized the importance of deliberately teaching students precise vocabulary through modeling, prompting, repetition, and sentence frames with the end goal of having students use precise language on their own.

Reflection Question

1. Have you explicitly differentiated between a formal academic register and other informal registers and dialects with your students?

Providing students with repeated exposure to an academic register requires constant reflection and analysis on the part of the teacher regarding his or her own language. The authors engaged teachers in a year-long series of ongoing professional-development sessions. Prior to the professional-development trainings, teachers were made aware of the focus of the new learning in the trainings and asked to respond to several questions in a presurvey.

Question 1 asked, How much of an impact do you think a teacher's choice of vocabulary has on students' language development?

	1	2	3	4	5	
Minimal Impact	○	○	○	○	○	Great Impact

All participants in the survey chose numbers four or five, indicating that teacher talk has a great impact on students' language development. Despite teachers' belief that their language choice impacts students' language development, their use of elevated language in classrooms revealed a different story.

Question 2, based on the HIERARCHY OF COMPETENCE (Burch, 1970), asked the following:

In which of the four bands of consciousness would you place yourself with respect to your current use of elevated teacher talk during delivering instruction, giving directions, and engaging in social conversations?

- Unconscious Competence: My new skills are second-nature and require little effort.
- Conscious Competence: I begin to apply my new skills, but it takes effort.

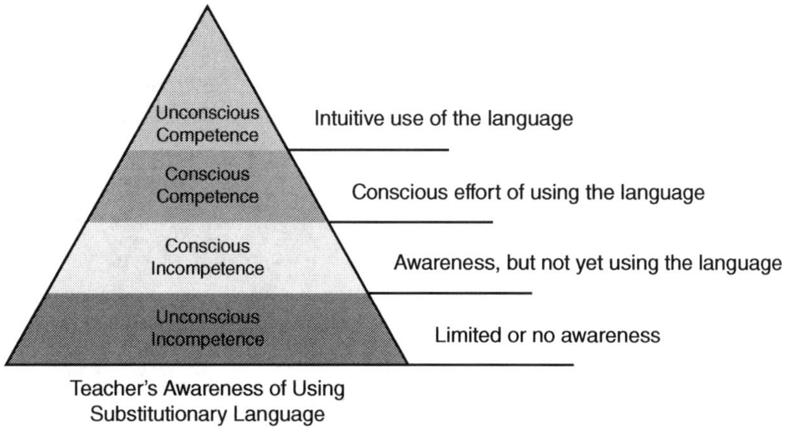

Figure 1.1 Teacher's Awareness of Using Substitutionary Language Adapted by Burch, 1970

- Conscious Incompetence: I begin to realize where I fall short.
- Unconscious Incompetence: I am unaware of what I don't know.

The survey results indicated that 83% of the participants identified themselves as either unconsciously competent or consciously competent. Although this percentage indicated that the majority of teachers self-reported that they were applying elevated language, either consciously or unconsciously, walk-throughs conducted prior to the trainings revealed otherwise. The researchers found that the majority of teachers were using academic language in their delivery of instruction. Few, however, were consistently speaking in an academic register with their students.

The authors' adaption of Burch's four stages of the HIERARCHY OF COMPETENCE aptly refers to the stages one goes through in applying the principle of substitutionary language. Simply defined, substitutionary language is the deliberate and systematic modeling on the part of teachers to replace their use of common words with more sophisticated and precise language, which will be discussed in more detail in Chapter 2. Many teachers, when first confronted with the importance of modeling robust language for students, assume that they are already putting this language into practice because they teach academic vocabulary and model it for their students. Elevated language is much more. It is modeling an academic register throughout the school day at the word, sentence, and discourse level. It is seizing every opportunity to model elevated language for our students.

Reflection Questions #2 and #3

2. Where do you believe you fall on the HIERARCHY OF COMPETENCE with respect to using the principle of substitutionary language? Explain. If you are brave, invite a peer into your classroom to evaluate your use of elevated language!

____

____

____

3. Author Lisa Delpit (2013) describes teachers who hold high expectations for their students and helps them see and reach their full potential as warm demanders. Now think back to Verplaetse (1998) and the Benevolent Conspiracy. All of us have a natural bent towards either demanding or inadvertently holding low expectations. Where do you fall?

____

____

____

References

Appel, R., & Muysken, P. (2005). *Language contact and bilingualism.* Amsterdam University Press.

Burch, N. (1970). *Conscious competence theory of learning a new skill.* www.mccc.edu/~lyncha/documents/stagesofcompetence.pdf

Delpit, L. (2006). *Other people's children: Cultural conflict in the classroom.* The New Press.

Delpit, L. (2013). *Multiplication is for white people: Raising expectations for other people's children.* The New Press.

Emdin, C. (2016). *For white folks who teach in the hood . . . and the rest of y'all too.* Beacon Press.

Filmore, C. J., & Filmore, L. W. (2012). *What does text complexity mean for English learners and language minority students?* Understanding Language: Stanford University School of Education.

Rowe, C., & Suarez, W. (2019). *Challenging English learners to improve academic discourse.* The Pennsylvania Administrator.

Verplaetse, L. S. (1998). How content teachers interact with English language learners. *TESOL Journal, 7*(5), 24–28.

2

The Principle of Substitutionary Language

Definition of Substitutionary Language

With so much on a teacher's daily plate, we are not talking about cramming additional lessons and activities that explicitly teach vocabulary and complex sentence structure into already jam-packed lesson plans. We are talking about deliberate "teacher talk." You know the saying "Think about what you say before you say it?" We are asking you to choose your words carefully, because teacher modeling is key. Check your speech; are you using the same words and phrases instead using a variety of them? Teacher talk is about the ability to seize every opportunity to build upon existing vocabularies and to use substitutionary language when possible. This is infused in everything we do, throughout the instructional day, in our daily routines and existing structure. In addition to using substitutionary language during instruction and while giving classroom procedures, we can use it while interacting with students on the playground, in the cafeteria, during study halls, and during interactions before and after school.

Consider, for example, the morning meeting routine. The teacher calls his or her students to the carpet to begin the morning ritual. Several actions may occur simultaneously. The teacher gives the command, "Please come to the carpet." As the command is given, the teacher also gestures with his or her hand, using a motion that conveys, *come*. The routine is quickly established as students' physical movement to the carpet is coupled with the gesture signaling students to move. Even English learners are able to grasp the meaning of

DOI: 10.4324/9781003295716-3

"Please come to the carpet" when it is supported with gestures that provide comprehensible input. It's quite possible that some teachers might use the same language in that sentence all year long. The result . . . students would come to the carpet; however, what a missed opportunity with respect to building language!

What Does the Research Say?

Children do not just soak up what goes on around them but actively try to make sense of the language they are exposed to (Gass & Selinker, 1994). As students receive the language, they will produce language by making generalizations and hypotheses. They will attempt to use words in a context and construct grammars. As the child has more exposure to the objects in different contexts, he/she will start to use precise language. It is important for teachers to know this information and use it as a springboard for teaching vocabulary both implicitly and explicitly. Once a student knows a word, that is the time for teachers to use substitutionary language.

The "Principle of Substitutionary Language," as coined by Haase and Rowe, denotes the idea that once children understand a word or a concept, even receptively, substituting synonyms for that word will bolster students' language. This concept is best understood through examples. Remember our earlier example of "Come to the carpet." Even newcomer English Learners (ELs) quickly come to understand its meaning, spoken by their teachers, when supported with the hand gesture "come." For many students, the verbal command "Come to the carpet" is heard on a daily basis as part of classroom routines. The Principle of Substitutionary Language suggests that as soon as students demonstrate understanding of a given vocabulary word or phrase, teachers should begin to replace those words with more sophisticated language. "Come to the carpet" becomes "Congregate on the carpet" and further expands to "Congregate on the rectangular carpet" to reinforce math academic vocabulary. Elevated language can be used wherever and whenever possible.

When implementing the Principle of Substitutionary Language, the authors suggest beginning with classroom procedures, as these are predictable situations, permitting the teacher to plan for opportunities of substituting language. Scores of imperatives spoken by teachers daily can provide an abundance of opportunities to bolster students' vocabularies. Environments outside of the classroom, such as the hallway, the cafeteria, and the playground, all provide additional opportunities for elevated verbal input.

The phrase "Be careful on the equipment" becomes "Exercise caution on the equipment." After students come in from the playground, instead of asking if they would like to get a drink of water, we could say, "Would you care to partake in a beverage at the water fountain?" Finally, instructional periods during the school day are also ripe with opportunities for teachers to model more sophisticated language.

The key for teachers to effectively use the Principle of Substitutionary Language is to continually reflect on the language they use throughout the school day. Teachers should ask the following questions: Where in my directions and routines can I begin to substitute synonyms using elevated language? How can I maximize my language in noninstructional settings, such as on the playground, where students are often socializing? And finally, in what ways can I provide opportunities for my students to hear elevated vocabulary reinforced during instruction? This simple yet powerful strategy of using substitutionary language can help build students' vocabularies exponentially when used consistently by teachers and established as part of a common school culture.

Now imagine the reflective, intentional teacher who is looking for every opportunity to grow students' vocabularies. "Please come to the carpet" becomes "Please congregate on the carpet." The gesture has remained the same, but the language has slightly changed, with one word being replaced by another. The teacher praises her students saying, "Good job, class. We've congregated on the carpet! Look at us all together, we have formed a congregation," she adds with a gesture implying *all together*.

So why is providing students opportunities to hear elevated language important? Our students, without a doubt, will hear the word "come" many times, in and out of school. The same cannot be said of a more sophisticated word such as "congregate." It is our job, as teachers, to provide rich opportunities to grow students' receptive vocabularies if we ever hope to have them produce the language in their speech and writing.

In addition, if students consistently listen to higher-level vocabulary, it increases the likelihood of them recognizing and comprehending the vocabulary when reading. Burkins and Yates (2021) stated:

> Every time you talk to students, you make choices about which words to share with them. Don't hesitate or shy away from using big, bold, audacious words. You don't have to water language down for children. Using strong vocabulary will not only make your kids feel respected, but once you've planted the seeds in students' phonological lexicons—where the brain collects every word it has ever heard—you've increased the chance that they will develop an understanding of it, try it out for themselves, and even recognize it when they encounter it in print.
>
> (p. 27)

Imagine, now, the students in a classroom in which their teacher consistently uses the principle of substitutionary language throughout the entire school year. This teacher's students will grow their vocabularies exponentially compared to those of the teacher who repeatedly uses entry-level, common vocabulary. Furthermore, when we use high-level vocabulary with our students on a regular basis, we are sending the message that we respect them and we have high expectations for them because we know they are capable. One former fifth-grade student expressed her approval of elevated language to Kristen, saying, "You're using such fancy words. It gets boring hearing teachers use the same words over and over every day."

Reflection Question

1. Let's take the wise counsel of Kristen's student and spice up the common words and phrases we use in the classroom. Consider how you typically praise students. If you are like most of us, you have your "go-to" quips, such as "Awesome!" and "Great job!" Those could be substituted with, "Very commendable!"

My Go-To Quips	My New Substitutionary Language

Let's review . . .

What Substitutionary Language Is	What Substitutionary Language Is Not
Implicit teaching	Explicit teaching
Used consistently and constantly	Used sporadically
Used while teaching a lesson	Written up in a lesson plan
Spoken throughout the entire school day	Spoken only during instruction
Used in context	Taught using vocabulary lists and in isolation

In order to optimize opportunities to bolster language in the classroom, teachers can refine their own talk in such a way that slang and colloquial language are minimized from their vocabularies and replaced with high-level language. That's empowering for students and teachers alike. This book offers strategies to implement in your classroom to ensure that all students have access to the same elevated vocabulary; this is equity. So let's get started!.

References

Burkins, J., & Yates, K. (2021). *Shifting the balance*. Stenhouse Publishers.

Gass, S., & Selinker, L. (1994). *Second language acquisition: An introductory course*. Lawrence Erlbaum Associates, Publishers.

3

The Importance of Oral Language Inside and Outside the Classroom

The Importance of Oral Language

Let's Break Down the Components of Language

There are four main components of language:

1. Phonology—the rules about the structure and sequence of speech sounds.
2. Semantics consists of vocabulary and how concepts are expressed through words.
3. Grammar involves two parts. Syntax is the rules in which words are arranged into sentences. Morphology is the use of grammatical markers (indicating tense, active or passive voice, etc.).
4. Pragmatics involves the rules for appropriate and effective communication.

The focus of this book will be mostly semantics, occasionally referencing pragmatics. We will discuss how to adjust teacher talk at the word level in order to build students' vocabulary and academic register. This chapter lays a foundation and provides the rationale. It is divided into three sections. In the first section, we will discuss the importance of oral language in the early childhood classroom, which is the ideal time for language growth. In the next section, we examine the research supporting the importance of oral language development in the area of literacy. We conclude by discussing the importance

DOI: 10.4324/9781003295716-4

of oral language in regard to our English language learners. By the end of this chapter, the reader will realize the imperativeness of using elevated language. This, in turn, will set the stage for all staff members of a school to examine their own speech in order to increase their students' academic register.

The Importance of Oral Language in Early Childhood

The 30-Million-Word Difference—Hart Risley Study

The students' vocabulary development begins before they set foot through the school doors. During early childhood, children learn vocabulary at the rate of approximately 2,000 to 4,000 words per year (Brabham & Villaume, 2002). Genishi states that parents, caregivers, teachers, and guardians are the chief resources in language development. Children learn much from each other, but adults are the main conversationalists, questioners, listeners, responders, and sustainers of language development and growth in the child-care center or classroom (Genishi, 1988).

Let us explore the importance of our words. The Hart and Risley (1995) study found that children from families receiving government assistance heard about 616 words per hour, while those from working-class families heard around 1,251 words per hour, and those from professional families heard roughly 2,153 words per hour. Thus, children from better financial circumstances had far more language exposure to draw from. The finding that children living in poverty hear fewer than a third of the words heard by children from higher-income families has significant implications in the long run. These results reveal a 30-million-word difference. That is, a child from a high-income family will experience 30 million more words within the first four years of life than a child from a low-income family. This gap does nothing but grow as the years progress, ensuring slow growth for children who are economically disadvantaged and accelerated growth for those from more privileged backgrounds.

In addition, the study found a wide disparity in the quantity of words (sum of unique words and gross sum of all words) as well as the quality of language to which the children were exposed. Children in families considered low socioeconomic status (SES) were exposed to short imperatives and typically negative words such as "No . . . Stop that." In contrast, children from high-SES families tended to be exposed to a greater quantity and quality of words. Their interactions included descriptive language, expansive narrations, and positive reinforcement for communication.

> While socioeconomics is a factor in this particular study, it is not the only factor. Let us focus on the amount of words students hear in early childhood and the quality of those words.

Reflection Questions

1. What are some of the implications of the research?

 ____

 ____

2. How could this research help to inform your strategic modeling of vocabulary in the early childhood classroom?

 ____

 ____

Conclusion

The authors recognize that not all young children have had the same language experiences and that they arrive at school with varying language repertoires. In addition, the authors believe the key to closing this language gap is teacher talk. The importance of teachers in early childhood classrooms using higher-level language is critical to closing this gap. Moreover, if teachers close the gap, students will be better prepared when they encounter the print-rich classrooms of elementary school. In 2009, the National Early Literacy Panel found a high correlation between preschool language skills and reading competence at the end of first and second grade. Other studies have shown that language in the preschool years predicts reading in the later elementary grades (e.g., fourth grade) and middle school (Dickinson & Porche, 2011). If multiple exposures to academic vocabulary are used by the teacher when students are at a young age, the students' vocabulary begins to expand so that when the opportunity comes to introduce the written word, the students will come with a word vault that will allow them access to the written word as well as comprehension of the meaning of the words. In conclusion, when children hear high quality adult speech and when they have had the fullest, freest opportunities to talk, they are being taught to read (Hymes, 1965).

The Impact of Oral Language on Fostering Literacy in the Classroom and Beyond

Let's start this section with some interesting facts:

- Only 10,000 different words account for about 96% of words in spoken English.
- The number of different words in popular contemporary print is at least 1,000,000.

- If conversational levels of spoken language were reflected in print, we would be limited to a reading level equivalent to grade 4 or below. Clearly, written language is more sophisticated, consistent, and exact than spoken language.

Reflection Questions

3. Are you surprised by this information?

___

___

___

4. What are the implications of these statistics?

___

___

___

With only 10,000 words being part of our oral discourse throughout the day and the number of words in print being close to a million, that leaves a gap of 990,000! In addition, most of us are conversing orally on a fourth-grade level and most newspapers are printed on a sixth-grade level. We must use the knowledge of these statistics to bolster our vocabularies so that we can bolster our students' vocabularies.

In regard to the literacy classroom, more and more research is emerging emphasizing the importance of oral language and its impact on reading. According to Wong Filmore and Snow (2000), oral language functions as a foundation for literacy and as the means of learning in school and out. However, despite its importance for learning, many teachers know much less about oral language than they need to know (Wong Filmore & Snow, 2000). Furthermore, the relationship between vocabulary and reading comprehension is thought to be reciprocal—knowing more words facilitates successful comprehension, while successful comprehension and wider reading lead to opportunities to learn more words (Stanovich, 1986). Therefore, a talk-rich environment in schools is imperative. Furthermore, with the emphasis of children reading in kindergarten, developing students' oral vocabulary is urgent. In our experiences, when an emphasis is placed on reading too quickly without giving students ample opportunity to make meaning out of language that occurs through listening and conversations, students may learn the written word; however, they will struggle with literacy comprehension. The research supports this notion. Children with a history of oral language impairment are more likely to present with reading difficulties than their peers (general population). Some research identified this difference to be as great as four to five times more likely than their peers (Catts et al., 2001).

As a result of this, we feel a strong call to action for teachers to increase their use of higher-level language in the classroom and beyond. In their book *Shifting the Balance: 6 Ways to Bring the Science of Reading Into the Balanced Literacy Classroom* (2021), Jan Burkins and Kari Yates state, "Teachers should not hesitate from using big, old, audacious words. You don't have to water language down for children." In their well-written article featured in Reading Rockets, Lane and Allen (2010) talk about the importance of using sophisticated words in the classroom to promote vocabulary growth. We couldn't agree more!

According to Nonie Lesaux, associate professor at the Harvard Graduate School of Education, vocabulary learning is an enormous task for all students; in order to be academically successful, students must leave high school with a working understanding of about 50,000 words. Now think back to research on the 30-million-word gap. What if teachers were able to shrink that gap by focusing on using higher-level vocabulary in their lessons, in their directives, and in their everyday interactions with the students?

Reflection Questions

Before listening to Nonie Lesaux's "A Matter of Talk," answer the following questions:

1. In your opinion, is the way in which we speak and the vocabulary we use connected to our reading ability? If so, in what ways?

   ____

   ____

2. Reflecting on the first question, do you feel the way you speak throughout your working day is connected to literacy in your classroom?

   ____

   ____

Now, answer questions 3 and 4 as you listen to "A Matter of Talk" by Nonie Lesaux from the Harvard Graduate School of Education. Lesaux (2014) delivered a speech on the topic of teacher talk, which she refers to as the "uncultivated, unattended-to lever for change." The speaker studied the impact of a teacher's complex words on student reading achievement in sixth-grade classrooms in an urban school district.

"A Matter of Talk" by Nonie Lesaux

During the Video

3. At about the 2:27 mark, you will see a chart. At first glance, what does that chart mean to you?

4. At approximately the 6:40 mark, she talks about the 20,000 hours of schooling a child receives. What are the implications of teacher talk throughout a child's school career?

After the video, answer questions 5 and 6:

5. Lesaux states it is not how much talk a teacher uses but rather the words the teacher uses. What are the implications of this statement on your teacher practice?

6. In the article, "Oral-Language Skills for English-Learners Focus of Researchers" (Zehr, 2009), Catherine E. Snow, a professor of education at the Harvard Graduate School of Education, stated that oral language is good for all students, "but the at-risk ones are totally dependent on schools to give it to them, while other kids can get it in other places" (p. 3). What are the implications of this on your teaching practice with respect to providing equitable access to at-risk students?

Conclusion

Oral language development plays a vital role in the literacy-rich classroom. In order to provide equitable access to the curriculum, teachers must close the word gap. In their article "Increasing Exposure to Academic Language by Speaking It" (Himmele & Himmele, 2009), Bill and Persida Himmele state that it is important to increase students' exposure to academic language by speaking it (p. 1). We need to expose students to words they may not hear outside the classroom if we expect them to be successful in the literacy classroom. They need to encounter higher-level words before they begin reading in order to have greater success comprehending the text.

The Importance of Oral Language for ELs

Check Your knowledge

1. Put the following four language skills in order of acquisition for how a child learns his or her first language.
   – Listening Writing Speaking Reading

1.	**3.**
2.	**4.**

2. Which are productive skills and which are receptive skills?

   ____

   ____

3. Rank the four language skills in order of importance in a fifth-grade classroom.

1.
2.
3.
4.

4. Reflect on your second-language experiences. Did you learn in a classroom? If so, how did you best learn?

   ____

   ____

   ____

5. Read this scenario and answer the questions below as they pertain to students' learning of additional languages.

Abedi is 7 years old and placed in second grade. She speaks Swahili but has not learned to read or write in Swahili. There are no students in her classroom who speak her native language. Her family is from a small village in Tanzania but was living in a refugee camp in Sudan until they were granted refugee status to come to the United States.

- How might she feel as she enters the classroom? ____________
- What does she hear? ______________________________
- ______________________________________
- What does she understand? ________________________
- What academic tasks can she do? ____________________
____
____

6. Have you ever traveled to a country in which your first language wasn't spoken? How did you get around? ________________
____
____
____
____
____

A Brief Look at the Role of Oral Language in Second-Language Acquisition

As English as a Second Language (ESL) teachers who have taught ELs from all over the world, we know the importance of oral language. Oral language plays an important role in language acquisition. Teachers' speech provides multiple exposures to language that is understandable, or comprehensible. That is the first step needed for beginning ELs to acquire vocabulary. Eventually, after many repetitions of hearing a word, students will take the risk to try the word in their own speech.

When newcomer students enter the schools, there is a period known as the silent period. During this stage, students are absorbing language, yet they are not producing much language. This stage could last for several weeks or longer, depending on the student. Teachers need to understand the silent period is part of the language acquisition process. During this time, it is important for the teacher to speak clearly, repeat words and phrases, and use gestures and other visuals to help understanding.

If students have language deficits in their first language, acquiring a second language is all the more challenging. As an example, if students have not learned to read and write in their first language, the challenge of learning to read in their second language will be greater. They do not have reading and writing strategies from which to pull; therefore, they will rely on their English vocabulary to help them. Thomas and Collier (1995) noted that students who lack prior schooling and who may have very weak or nonexistent primary-language skills may require from 7 to 10 years to master academic language.

A Question From the Field

You have been talking about the importance of using academic and elevated language in the classroom; however, if I have newcomers such as Abedi in my classroom, should I use elevated language with them?

This is a question teachers often ponder. We like to explain that we follow Stephen Krashen's rule of $i + 1$. We travel along this continuum by receiving what Stephen Krashen (1982, 1985) termed "comprehensible input." Comprehensible input is input that is slightly beyond the current level of competence of the language learner. If i is the language learner's current level of competence in English, then $i + 1$ is the next immediate step along the development continuum. For example, if the student understands the concept of a ball, we can start introducing different types of balls, describing the shape of the ball using words such as "round" or "sphere." Therefore, after your student has a solid understanding of a word or concept, you can use substitutionary language.

A Point to Ponder

English learners start their learning underground, while native English speakers are aboveground. If the learner has an understanding of the word or concept in his/her home language, the student simply needs to translate the word and now is aboveground. However, if the student is unfamiliar with the concept or the word in his/her native language, the student will remain underground until the word or concept is understood. You can see how students may stay underground for long periods of time and need multiple tools to help them get to level ground.

For school-aged children, acquiring English means not only developing basic command of the language but also understanding the academic vocabulary used in school texts (Stanovich, 1986). Second-language acquisition researchers who study language-proficiency development of second-language students make a distinction between language that is used for basic social interaction and language that is needed for meeting the challenges of academic coursework and communication (Cummins, 1979). Basic interpersonal communication skills are language skills needed for daily conversational purposes, whereas cognitive academic language proficiency refers to the vocabulary students encounter in academic texts. This is also the register students need to use when writing academic papers. Peregoy and Boyle (2000) went on to suggest that students might demonstrate basic social competence in a second language within 6 months to 2 years after arrival in a new country. The skills related to talking with friends or managing daily affairs cannot be equated with the ability to comprehend and express oneself where knowledge of academic vocabulary is required (Thomas & Collier, 1995). Teachers often question why ELs are not performing well on academic tasks. Understanding the research offers some insight to why that might be the case. Adding to the challenge, differences in both vocabulary knowledge and reading outcomes between native speakers and language-minority learners have been shown to widen over time (Lesaux et al., 2010).

Conclusion

Oral language is a key component of second-language acquisition. ELs need to develop oral language in English in order to be successful in the academic classroom. As educators, we must understand that all English language learners do not fit the same mold, and acquiring academic English can take years. Furthermore, students with limited formal schooling face more challenges acquiring English than students who are literate in their first language. However, developing a strong oral vocabulary will assist ELs in accessing the curriculum. While students are developing their command of social English, teachers can start to infuse substitutionary language into their own speech. In many cases, English language learners plateau in their English proficiency due to a lack of exposure to and command of academic vocabulary. We can prevent this by understanding our students' language acquisition process and providing them with access to elevated language as they progress up the proficiency scale.

References

Brabham, E. G., & Villaume, S. K. (2002). Vocabulary instruction: Concerns and visions. *Reading Teacher*, *56*(3), 264–268.

Burkins, J., & Yates, K. (2021). *Shifting the balance*. Stenhouse Publishers.

Catts, H. W., Fey, M. E., Zhang, X., & Tomblin, J. B. (2001). Estimating the risk of future reading difficulties in kindergarten children: A research-based model and its clinical implementation. *Language, Speech, and Hearing Services in Schools, 32*(1), 38–50. doi:10.1044/0161-1461(2001/004). PMID: 27764435.

Cummins, J. (1979). *Cognitive/academic language proficiency, linguistic interdependence, the optimum age question and some other matters*. Working Papers on Bilingualism, No. 19, 121–129.

Dickinson, D. K., & Porche, M. V. (2011). Relation between language experiences in preschool classrooms and children's kindergarten and fourth-grade language and reading abilities. *Child Development, 82*(3), 870–886. www.jstor.org/stable/29782878

Genishi, C. (1988). Children's language: Learning words from experience. *Young Children, 44*(1), 16–23. www.jstor.org/stable/42728549

Hart, B., & Risley, T. R. (1995). *Meaningful differences in the everyday experience of young American children*. Paul H. Brookes Publishing Company.

Himmele, B., & Himmele, P. (2009). Increasing exposure to academic language by speaking it. *ASCD, 5*(5).

Hymes, J. L., Jr. (1965). Early reading is very risky business. *Grade Teacher, 82*, 88–92.

Krashen, S. (1982). *Principles and practice in second language acquisition*. Pergamon.

Krashen, S. (1985). *The input hypothesis: Issues and implications*. Longman.

Lane, H. B., & Allen, S. A. (2010). The vocabulary-rich classroom: Modeling sophisticated word use to promote word consciousness and vocabulary growth. *Reading Teacher, 63*(5), 362–370.

Lesaux, N. (2014). *A matter of talk*. Harvard Graduate School of Education.

Lesaux, N., Kieffer, M. J., Faller, S. E., & Kelley, J. G. (2010). The effectiveness and ease of implementation of an academic vocabulary intervention for linguistically diverse students in urban middle schools. *Reading Research Quarterly, 45*(2), 196–228. doi:10.1598/RRQ.45.2.3

National Institute for Literacy. (2009). *Shanahan, T. & Lonigan, C. Developing early literacy: Report of the national early literacy panel*. Executive Summary. A Scientific Synthesis of Early Literacy Development and Implications for Intervention.

Peregoy, S. F., & Boyle, O. F. (2000). English learners reading English: What we know, what we need to know. *Theory into Practice, 39*(4), 237–247.

Stanovich, K. E. (1986). Matthew effects in reading: Some consequences of individual differences in the acquisition of literacy. *Reading Research Quarterly, 21*, 360–407. http://dx.doi.org/10.1598/RRQ.21.4.1

Thomas, W. P., & Collier, V. (1995). *Research summary of study in progress: Results as of September 1995, language minority student achievement and program effectiveness*. National Clearinghouse for Bilingual Education.

Wong Filmore, L., & Snow, C. E. (2000). *What teachers need to know about language*. The Center for Applied Linguistics.

Zehr, M. A. (2009). *Oral-language skills for English-learners focus of researchers*. Education Week.

4

Strategies for Implementing Substitutionary Language

Where Do I Start?

In this chapter, we will roll up our sleeves and do the important work of reflecting on our current teacher talk and develop a game plan for consistently using an academic register throughout the day and exposing all students to rich vocabulary in our sentences and discourse, across all content areas. We will:

- Eliminate the less formal aspects of our speech.
- Develop a plan for using academic vocabulary across the content areas.
- Gain tools for bolstering our teacher talk at the word, sentence, and discourse levels.
- Explore strategies that aid our students' comprehension of elevated academic vocabulary.

Also included are tips for implementing the strategy with ELs, as well as insights for working with elementary and secondary students.

DOI: 10.4324/9781003295716-5

Strategy #1: Ridding Ourselves of Informal Language

Strategy Focus

Modeling an academic register begins with an awareness of our informal contractions, filler words, and ambiguous language. This chapter helps teachers become aware of the presence of this informal language in our speech. We can do this by listening to ourselves. Recording our speech works best, as we can listen somewhat more objectively than trying to analyze our speech in real time. Readers will identify informal language usages and then begin the conscientious elimination of them.

Strategy #1: Ridding Ourselves of Informal Language

For my student teaching experience, I taught high school Spanish. One day at the end of the class, a student who never participated raised his hand. I was so thrilled! He was finally going to speak some Spanish! I called on him and he said, "Senorita, you said 'OK' 75 times during class today!"

~Kristen Haase, former Spanish teacher and current ELD Teacher

Introduction

Informal contractions, such as "hasta," "gonna," and "could've" are perfectly acceptable in everyday speech; however, academic settings demand more formal language. Nondescript nouns such as "things" and "stuff" are also acceptable in social conversation, but in academic circles, we need to use precise language to be sure our messages are communicated accurately. In addition, teachers often use "okay" and "like" during transition times, as seen in the quote above. As a time saver, teachers often ask questions like "Which one? or "How many?" In her article "Cutting to the Common Core: Disrupting Discourse" (2018), Kate Kinsella states, "We pose vague questions with imprecise terms such as "What's your idea? Does anyone want to share? Instead, we should be framing our questions very deliberately" (p. 6). If the students are uncertain of the context, they will be confused and need to ask follow-up questions which would have been unnecessary had the teacher used more precise language.

Description of the Strategy

The strategy of eliminating informal language from our everyday speech recognizes teachers use words which are nondescript and are not found in most academic texts. Most of us are using these words unconsciously and habitually.

Students hear these words or phrases in social situations and are often familiar with them. For example, a student may hear the word "cuz" multiple times throughout the day while they are talking to their friends or even adults. The reflective teacher can eliminate these words from their repertoire if they become consciously aware of the use of these words throughout their day.

Rationale

What do students need to know? Think back to our first chapter: "Prepared for Life." Our students will master social language with their peers; however, they will need to be able to code-switch by using academic language and more precise vocabulary in the career and college worlds. The language of academics is precise, rigorous, and often not commonly heard in everyday speech. How do we expect our students to master the language of academics if they are only seeing it in textbooks? Furthermore, students will most likely not be permitted to use this type of informal language in their papers, and this language is not found in written form in the workplace.

What's the challenge? Students are most familiar with informal language. They hear it outside of school, when they are talking and texting with their friends, and in the classroom. Informal register is everywhere and habitual. Most people do not speak like Moira Rose from *Schitt's Creek* and Frasier and Niles Crane from the '90s hit show *Frasier*. People do not want to sound too highbrow and pompous. Teachers want to be able to connect with their students and speak informally at times in order to do that.

Using vague language can often cause confusion and frustration on the part of both the listener and the speaker. Oftentimes, vague language opens the door to interpretation on the part of the listener, allowing for the message to be interpreted incorrectly. Moreover, the listener may become more passive because the speaker is not being direct. The listener concludes the message is not important and, as a result, tunes out the speaker.

What does the strategy offer? Remember Verplaetse's (1998) phrase the "Benevolent Conspiracy." We cannot inadvertently lower expectations. As teachers, we have an incredible opportunity to grow our students' vocabulary by exposing them to the elevated language they will need to be successful in the classroom and beyond. As educators, we can make a conscious effort to reduce informal language from our speech and substitute more precise language, thereby growing our students' vocabulary. By using precise and descriptive language, we can avoid miscommunication. We can avoid follow-up questions and redirection because the students will know precisely what we are asking. In addition, by eliminating "filler words" such as "like" and "okay," we can sound more like the language of textbooks and formal writing.

Ideas in Action

Before we try our hand at our first substitutionary language strategy, take time to complete the elimination activity below:

1. Access your recording (prereading activity). Listen to your recording of giving directions in its entirety. Record any first impressions and observations below. ______________________________
____
____
____

2. Listen to your recording a second time. Place a checkmark beside any informal contractions each time you hear them. Speaking in an academic register includes eliminating these types of contractions from our teacher talk.

	a lotta = a lot of		gotta = got to		lemme = let me		shoulda = should have
	cuz = because		hafta = have to		needa = need to		tellem = tell them
	gimme = give me		hasta = has to		oughta = ought to		wanna = want to
	gonna = going to		kinda = kind of		outta = out of		whatcha = what are you

Before you listen to your recording a third time, study the chart that follows.

Nondescriptive Words/Phrases and Vague Modifiers

1		Things		stuff		Okay		like (as a filler word, not using figurative language)
2		over there (with no context or gestures)		that one (with no context or gestures)		this one (with no context or gestures)		her/him/it/they (with no context or gestures)
3		Many		a lot		Soon		Most
4		kind of		sort of		a little bit		About

3. Listen to your recording a third time. Identify the presence of "filler words" such as "OK," "um," "so," and "like" and nondescript or vague language such as "things," "stuff," "over there," "that one." Identify the use of vague modifiers such as "soon," "a lot," etc. While these words are not necessarily considered informal language, they are nondescript and can open themselves up to interpretation and confusion. Record any that you used here:__________________

____

____

Reflection Questions

For questions 4 through 6, reflect on your teacher talk throughout the school day over the course of a few days.

4. Did you regularly use words and phrases from the charts?

____

____

5. Do you notice that you use informal language more during certain times of the day?

____

____

6. Did you notice yourself using any other words repeatedly in addition to the words listed? (Subsequent chapters will address how to substitute nuanced words for more common ones.)

____

____

Beginning the Work of Strategic Modeling

Make a conscientious effort to eliminate vague pronouns, nondescript language, and ambiguous adjectives, such as shown in the chart. Replace these with precise words and phrases. See the examples that follow.

Vague Language	He saw her.	Kevin saw Evelyn.
Nondescript	Put your extra **stuff** on the table.	Put your uneaten food on the share table beside the door.

Vague Language	He saw her.	Kevin saw Evelyn.
Demonstrative Adjectives	Get the ball **over there**.	Locate the ball adjacent to the gaga ball pit.
Vague Modifiers	We have **a lot** of work to do today.	We need to complete a myriad of tasks today, such as our math assessment, as well as finish our opinion pieces.

Now it is your turn. Complete this chart with examples like the ones listed. Notice the locations have changed, so you will need to think of the language used in those areas.

In the Classroom

Vague Language		
Nondescript		
Demonstrative Adjectives		
Vague Modifiers		

In the Cafeteria

Vague Language		
Nondescript		
Demonstrative Adjectives		
Vague Modifiers		

On the Playground

Vague Language		
Nondescript		
Demonstrative Adjectives		
Vague Modifiers		

Conclusion

The goal of the preceding activities is for you to become more conscious of the words you use in your everyday speech. Although you only recorded a small snippet of your speech, we hope this serves as a springboard to further examination of every interaction you have with students. Noticing is an important first step. Remember the importance of being consciously competent (Chapter 1). Now, you can begin the process of eliminating vague language from your speech and adding more descriptive words through strategic modeling. The strategies in the upcoming chapters will assist you in this mindset shift.

References

Kinsella, K. (2018). Cutting to the common core: Disrupting discourse. *Language Magazine,* January 30, 2018.

Verplaetse, L. S. (1998). How content teachers interact with English language learners. *TESOL Journal, 7*(5), 24–28.

Strategy #2: Using Substitutionary Language While Giving Directions

Strategy Focus

As our classrooms get started at the beginning of the school year, among teachers' first considerations is establishing routines. Oftentimes, this includes giving specific directions and repetitive phrases, sentences, and discourse that will help facilitate teaching, foster security among students, and save time. The routines in this chapter are the perfect starting place for implementing substitutionary language.

Strategy #2: Using Substitutionary Language While Giving Directions

Introduction

Consider again the reflective teacher who intentionally substitutes the word "congregate" for "come" when calling his or her students to the carpet. It is a small change in the teacher's own talk, but after many repetitions, using the principle of substitutionary language, students will not only recognize the word when they hear it but will understand its meaning as well.

Description of the Strategy

This strategy will help teachers get started integrating elevated language into their speech. Because classroom procedures, directions, and routines are predictable, this is a good starting place for teachers wishing to implement substitutionary language. Teachers start by substituting one word in a sentence and then slowly, over time, continue to replace additional words with elevated language in order to bolster students' vocabularies.

Rationale

What do students need to know? Our students have been charged with achieving the rigorous academic standards that require them to comprehend and produce precise language. Giving directions provides dedicated time every day, multiple times a day, for using elevated language. During a conversation with her second-grade students, Jeanne Oakes stated during a class meeting on the use of sophisticated words, *"If I don't use them, how are you ever going to learn them?"* (J. Oakes, personal communication, April 11, 2022).

What's the challenge? We often speak using a more casual register and then expect students to engage in literacy skills in which they will be expected to read and write complex texts using an academic register. According to

Kate Kinsella (2018), transitioning from processing verbal directions posed in familiar social register to digesting written directions and texts framed in sophisticated academic register is tantamount to a linguistic whiplash. This provides a disconnect for our students as well as a missed opportunity to acquire rich, elevated academic language. Kinsella (2018) concurred on the matter of using elevated language when giving directions: "It becomes all the more vital for teachers to serve as proficient and unswerving academic language models" (p. 3).

What does the strategy offer? This strategy maximizes the use of directions that can be heard countless times throughout the school day. Since many directions are given on a routine basis, this strategy allows teachers and staff to plan for the use of substitutionary language.

The strategy offers an opportunity for teachers to bolster their students' language without incorporating explicit vocabulary and language instruction into their lesson plans. This chapter also lays the foundation for the reader to make a mindset shift toward using substitutionary language in every student interaction.

Ideas in Action

Carmen and Kristen feel the best place to start using substitutionary language is with directives. It is important for the readers to write their ideas down before putting the ideas into action so they have time to reflect and process the information. Veteran third-grade teacher Lenore Charnock has always tried to use higher-level vocabulary when communicating with her students. This is the way she spoke to her daughter and now speaks to her granddaughter. She would substitute a word here and there; however, after a professional-development series on substitutionary language by the authors, she became more intentional in her practice.

After a few days of practicing student routines in the beginning of the school year, Lenore likes to use substitutionary language when she gives directions. First, she started with simple directions the students have heard hundreds of times since they have come to school. Lenore started replacing the verbs in her commands. "Get out your . . ." was substituted with "Locate your . . . ." "Go to . . ." became "Travel, meander, or wander to . . . ." She makes sure she uses different nouns and verbs so that her speech does not become stagnant. Heeding the authors' advice, she took caution in not replacing too many words too quickly, before students have mastered the meaning of the new words. After a few weeks, she was consciously competent, making an effort to use substitutionary language when giving directions. (See Teacher's Awareness of Using Substitutionary Language chart in Chapter 1.)

Reflection Questions

1. Think of some directions you give repeatedly. What is one example?

 ____

 ____

2. What is one word you could substitute? Consider action verbs and common nouns.
 Rewrite the directive here.

 ____

 ____

The following chart proposes several scenarios for how you might implement the principle of substitutionary language when giving directions.

Directive	Directive With Substitutionary Language *Try...*	Rationale: How will bolstering our teacher talk while giving directions benefit students? *Why...*
Find your seat.	• Locate your seat. • Find your assigned destination.	• Using the verb "locate" in place of "find" exposures students to Tier 2 math vocabulary. (Locate the coordinates.) • Using the noun "destination" to describe where students are going or where they are being sent opens the door to teaching word families such as "destiny" and "destined."
Come to the carpet.	• Congregate on the carpet. • Come to the rectangular carpet.	• "Congregate" is a root word and will establish the foundation for other forms in this word family ("congregation," "congregants," "congregational"). • The use of "rectangular," a math academic vocabulary word, will be reinforced when used in context.

Directive	**Directive With Substitutionary Language** ***Try . . .***	**Rationale: How will bolstering our teacher talk while giving directions benefit students?** ***Why . . .***
Work with your elbow buddy.	• Work cooperatively with the classmate whose desk is adjacent to yours. • Work cooperatively with the classmate whose desk is contiguous to yours.	• "Cooperatively" will give them background knowledge of other words in this word family ("cooperation," "co-op"). • "Adjacent" describes location and will help prepare students for this term later in geometry. • "Contiguous" is a Tier 2 word often used in social studies or history to describe connecting states or countries.

1. Complete the chart that follows.
   In Column 1: Brainstorm three common commands that you routinely use in class. Write them in the form of sentences. Use the following questions as a guide:
   1. What activities do you typically ask students to start or stop?
   2. What materials will the students need?
   3. Where in the room should students be working?
   4. How will students complete the activity? Independently? In pairs? In small groups?

   ***Underline one word you will substitute with elevated language.
   In Column 2: Rewrite the sentence with the underlined word replaced with a more robust word.
   In Column 3: Note how this substitution will benefit your students. This is an important step! Understanding the "why" of this process will motivate you to continue in this work.

Directive With Simple Language ***Instead of . . .***	**Directive With Substitutionary Language** ***Try . . .***	**Rationale: How will this ratcheted-up language benefit your students?** ***Why? . . .***

2. Finally, listen to your recording again and complete the chart that follows.

   In Column 1: Write two sentences from your recorded directions. Underline one word from each sentence that you would consider simple, or basic, language.
   In Column 2: Rewrite the sentences, replacing the basic words with more elevated language.
   In Column 3: Explain the benefit of using this elevated language for students.

Directive With Simple Language ***Instead of...***	**Directive With Substitutionary Language** ***Try...***	**Rationale: How will this ratcheted-up language benefit your students?** ***Why?...***

Once you have become adept at substituting common words for more academic terms, you can start trying your hand at using substitutionary language for multiple words within a sentence as well as adding less commonly used parts of speech, such as adverbs. Now, take our directions a step farther. While giving directions should be concise and direct, using substitutionary language is imperative as well. Adding an adverb while giving directions will not only give the students an opportunity to hear a part of speech they don't often hear, but it will provide precise language that is often missing from directions.

Let's take a look at a simple way to do that. Below is a chart with commonly used verbs that are often heard on the school campus. On the right side of the chart are some adverbs we could add to our speech.

Adding Adverbs to Your Directives	
Write	neatly, legibly,
Walk	directly, calmly, cautiously, briskly
Read	silently, voraciously, clearly
Line up	quietly, immediately,
Speak	audibly, candidly, boldly

Use the space here to rewrite a few of the directives with adverbs.

1. ______________________________
2. ______________________________
3. ______________________________

Next Steps

Put your ideas into practice over the course of a week. After you have consistently used these directives with your students, ask and answer the following questions:

1. Were your students able to understand and follow your directives?

   ____

2. Were you able to use these directives with consistency?

   ____

3. What did you notice about the process?

   ____

Whatever your answers, they show you are consciously competent. You are now aware of making adjustments to your speech. This is an ongoing process.

Fast-forward to a few years later, and Lenore believes she is unconsciously competent using substitutionary language when giving many types of directions. Whether she is in the classroom, out on the playground, or walking her students down the hall, a casual observer notices her using elevated language with her students. When her students ask for clarification about directions, she will reword her commands; however, she will substitute with another higher-level vocabulary word.

As a co-teacher of Lenore, Kristen hears her in action every day when they conduct math rotations. At the end of each rotation, Lenore signals that the rotation has "terminated," and the students are to "Travel quietly to their next spot with the appropriate materials." She continues to find new ways of incorporating robust language in her directions given throughout the day.

Following is an additional opportunity to think about ways to incorporate elevated language in everyday directions. Remember: This is implicit teaching more than an explicit opportunity to teach vocabulary. Complete the following chart, substituting a word or phrase for the words at the top of the column.

Travel	Quietly	Spot	Materials

After you have completed the chart, write sentences you will use when giving directions.

1. ____
2. ____

Tips for ELs

Bolstering Teacher Talk With Student Buy-In

In order to put flesh and bones on the concept of using elevated language when giving directions, the authors met with elementary ESL teachers Jeanne Oakes and Yara Graupera. They both had expressed interest in the work the authors had done around bolstering teacher talk through strategic modeling in other schools. The authors met with them to devise a plan to jump-start the use of elevated language in their classrooms and in the classrooms in which they co-teach around language associated with giving directions. Carmen and Kristen suggest likening the use of elevated language to the way high school or college students speak when introducing the topic. In this way, younger learners feel empowered when using elevated language.

The mission of bolstering teacher talk was carried out using these four steps:

Step 1: Enlisting Students' Help

Jeanne and Yara began by telling their students that they had recently learned about the importance of using elevated language in their speech. They chose the phrase "fancy language" to introduce the concept, as it was a phrase that students had heard in previous lessons. Most of the students had heard the word "fancy" from the Fancy Nancy books written and illustrated by Jane O'Connor and Robin Preiss Glasser, which the teachers read regularly. Yara reinforced the concept of lifelong learning by saying, "Did you know that teachers never stop learning?" They went on to say that they would need their students' help in reminding them to use elevated language.

Figure 4b.1 Using Opposites on a Continuum

Figure 4b.2 Using Opposites on a Continuum During a Read Aloud

Jeanne explained to her first-grade students that she attended classes on how to use elevated language. She informed her students, "All of your teachers, myself included, need to start using fancy, academic words, so that you learn those words, too. We know many college words, but sometimes when we're speaking to you, we forget to use them. And if we don't use them, how are you ever going to learn them? Maybe all of you could help me use the fancy words. Who would be willing to help me?" To this question, all of her students' hands went up immediately, indicating buy-in. Yara used a similar approach with her students, adding, "My teacher told me that I need to use fancier words with all of you. But here's the problem . . . I'm so used to using the words I already know that I forget to use the fancy words. So your job is to say, 'Ms. Graupera, there's a fancier word for that."

Step 2: Recognizing Elevated Language in Speech and Text

Both Jeanne and Yara introduced the concept of using elevated language with their students using a picture book from the series Fancy Nancy. The main character not only wears fancy clothes but also uses fancy words. Yara prepares her students for reading by reminding them to be on the lookout for robust language. Then, before beginning the book, she tells students to hold up a finger if they hear a fancy word. Given a task, her students listen closely as she reads, holding up a finger when she says a fancy word.

While the Fancy Nancy books are a good starting place, the authors suggest teachers continue fostering a noticing of new words among their students. This practice can and should take place whenever and wherever new robust words are encountered, such as in read-alouds, during class discussions, while watching video clips, in texts, and any other opportunities.

Step 3: Anchor Chart Reminders

Jeanne and Yara both used anchor chart reminders of the robust words they should be modeling for students. They started modeling elevated language around the common verbs "go" and "stop" used when giving directives. Jeanne explains to her students that when she forgets to use a fancy word, they can look at the poster and say, "Ms. Oakes, you should use ________instead." She and her students have a conversation around the plain and fancy words.

The word "dispense" ignited some interesting conversation. Jeanne told a group of first-grade students she wasn't sure some college students knew this word, to which her students reacted with excitement, "Oooh!" The first-grade classroom teacher Barb Heister added, "What do we call the thing hanging in the bathroom, because I think that dispenses something? What is it called? A soap . . . dispenser! It passes out the soap" (B. Hesiter, personal communication, April 11, 2022).

Plain Words	Fancy Words
Get your supplies.	Collect your supplies.
	Gather your supplies.
Pass out the papers.	Distribute the papers.
	Dispense the papers.

Yara begins with two commonly used verbs, "go" and "stop." Using Carmen's "Opposites on a Continuum" activity cited in Strategy #3, Yara uses index cards on which she writes the verbs. She places the word "go" to her left and the word "stop" to her right. She then asks her students if these are fancy words. "No!" her students respond in unison. "I use these words a lot. I say, 'Go get your book.' 'Go to the nurse.' 'Stop at the door.' I use those words all the time, and they're just not fancy enough." One by one, Yara introduced the sophisticated vocabulary, and together with her students, they decided where to place them on the continuum. The diagram below is the chart her class created based on their conversation.

Step 4: Put it into Practice!

Put it into practice! Yara reminds her students, "If I say, 'Go to your seats.' You'll need to say, 'Ms. Graupera, "go" isn't a fancy word. I think you should use the word __________." As she paused, her students completed her sentence with, "proceed." Jeanne created the tabletop posters that serve as a visual reminder for students to use the new "college" vocabulary.

The authors use "verbal clozes" to reinforce new vocabulary with students. This is similar to written clozes in which a word is omitted for students to complete, but in this case, it is done orally. Students typically catch on

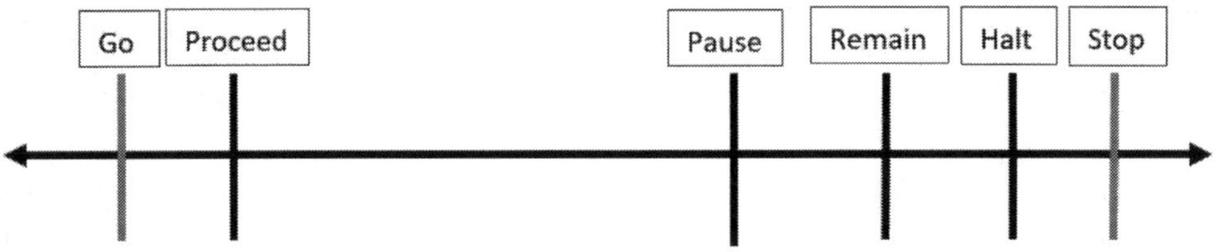

Figure 4b.3 Opposites on a Continuum

to this strategy, especially when teachers slow their speech and inflect their voice before the missing word. Following are a couple of examples:

- When we get to the water fountain, ____________________. Then resume walking down the hall.
- When we get to the water fountain, halt. Then ____________________ walking down the hall.

In a conversation with Carmen and Kristen, Jeanne pointed out that acknowledging students' attempts at using an academic register in their speaking and writing is important. "The classroom teacher and I seized upon the student's use of elevated language and celebrated it with the class in hopes that it might become contagious and promote it." Jeanne believes, "It is key that you celebrate when they even have an approximation to the correct use of the word" (J. Oakes, personal communication, April 11, 2022).

Jeanne also shared an anecdote of one first grader who tried to immediately use the new language. "While students were getting ready to go home, they were all running around. The young student held up a pencil and asked, 'Whoever's pencil this is, come and gather it.' The student had used the wrong word in this case. Nevertheless, Jeanne praised her for trying to use the word and modeled the correct word one-on-one for the student. The student, in turn, revised her question: 'Whoever's pencil this is, come and collect it.'" Yara, too, shared an anecdote. Students were in the library, being quite noisy. A student prodded Yara and said, "You should say, 'halt.'" Both teachers noted that students were very eager to try the language on; even if the approximations were off, they are using it.

Leah Flick, third-grade teacher, shared the following story. At the conclusion of a school assembly, a teacher asked students to "Assemble in a line and proceed to your classrooms." In response to this command, a student in Leah's classroom responded, "That teacher is using sophisticated language!" (L. Flick, personal communication, April 11, 2022).

Barb Heister encourages teachers to continue modeling elevated language in order to bolster vocabulary for all students, including ELs. She

Figure 4b.4 Table Top Poster

shared this story (B. Heister, personal communication, April 11, 2022): A young student came to her at the beginning of the school year only speaking Karen, a language spoken in Thailand, and is now speaking and communicating well in English. "One day, after introducing the sophisticated words and vocabulary, we were lining up at the end of the day, and I said, 'Friends, you need to get your things and get in line to get ready to go home.' The young student came up to me and said, 'Excuse me, Mrs. Heister, don't you mean "gather your things and proceed to the line"?' " Barb's story highlights the importance of providing access to elevated

Figure 4b.5 Cognate Support Poster

language for all students. With repeated exposure, students will come to understand the vocabulary and begin to use it in their own speech.

Cognates can be used to aid English learners' ability to decode the roots of unfamiliar English words and, in turn, bolster their understanding of English vocabulary and reading comprehension (Goodwin et al., 2012). Leah Flick also shared an accommodation for ELs she uses in her room, suggested by ESL teacher Yara Graupera. As noted in the chart in Figure 4b.5, Spanish cognates have been added to aid the ELs in her class, the majority of whom are Spanish speakers. This anchor poster serves several purposes. First, it reminds students of the fancy word choices they and their teachers have available. Second, the cognates provide Spanish-speaking students with comprehensible input. Finally, it raises everyone's awareness of the concept of cognates, Spanish speakers and non–Spanish speakers alike.

References

Goodwin, A., Lipsky, M., & Ahn, S. (2012). Word detectives: Using units of meaning to support literacy. *Reading Teacher*, *65*(7), 461–470. https://doi.org/10.1002/TRTR.01069

Kinsella, K. (2018). Cutting to the common core: Disrupting discourse. *Language Magazine*, January 30, 2018.

Strategy #3: Substituting More Nuanced Words and Phrases for Common Ones

Strategy Focus

Without a doubt, casual English has its favorite words and phrases. For example, some common verbs are "said," "come," and "go," to mention a few. Although these verbs fare well in everyday speech, they fall short of the rich, nuanced language required in narrative discourse and other formal types of writing. Modeling a rich variety of verbs for students builds their own repertoires of oral language and pays rich dividends in their writing as well.

Strategy #3: Substituting More Nuanced Words and Phrases for Common Ones

An important goal of all teachers is to continually model elevated language for students in order to expose them to a vast array of words with nuanced meanings. As students gain exposure to robust vocabulary they will be better equipped not only to comprehend precise language when reading, but also to express it in their thoughts in speaking and writing.

~Dr. Carmen Shahadi Rowe

Introduction

We hope that after dipping your toes in Strategies #1 and #2, you realize the importance of bolstering your teacher talk through strategic modeling and are becoming aware of the many opportunities throughout the school day to do this. A good place to start is with simple action verbs and adjectives. Action verbs are among the most basic parts of speech that students encounter. They are present in almost every simple sentence. Consider the verbs "said," "talk," and "walk." We, along with our students, use them on a daily basis. Oftentimes, we use any one of these verbs in a broad way to cover many meanings. Take for example the verb "talk." A student may be whispering during a quiet activity. We teachers might say, "Stop talking, please," when the student, to be precise, was whispering. The generalization of action verbs is a missed opportunity to model the use of similar but nuanced verbs.

Description of the Strategy

The chart that follows shows the verbs "said," "talk," and "walk" and how they might be substituted to convey more precise meaning. Teachers can introduce these nuanced meanings throughout the school day as they catch students whispering, chattering, and even perhaps murmuring. Coupling the use of these action verbs with a demonstration of what it looks and sounds like will help make the new vocabulary comprehensible to students.

While explaining that "a murmur is an indistinct sound of someone talking" will help students understand the meaning, demonstrating murmuring can provide an additional opportunity for students to understand the new vocabulary. The teacher can further reinforce this meaning as opportunities arise: "I hear someone murmuring. I can't hear exactly what they're saying, but I do hear talking."

Rationale

What do students need to know? The language of textbooks is much more rigorous and unfamiliar to students than the oral language and conversation they participate in throughout their day. If students are to be successful in the language of academics, they need to be exposed to the language of textbooks continuously throughout their day.

What's the challenge? In our experience, most language heard throughout a student's day is more conversational, basic, or social English. Oral language proficiency underscores advanced academic literacy (August & Shanahan, 2006). Therefore, we can conclude that students whose academic oral language proficiency is limited will struggle to read complex academic text.

What does the strategy offer? This strategy offers an opportunity for teachers to bolster their vocabulary by replacing more nuanced words for common ones. This strategy builds upon the last strategy but expands the scope of using substitutionary language. After focusing on bolstering their speech while giving directions, teachers can start looking for other opportunities throughout the day to use elevated language.

Ideas in Action

A good starting place is with common verbs. Consider the common verbs "said," "read," and "walk" in the chart that follows and their corresponding nuanced meanings.

Action Verbs & Nuanced Meanings		
Verb	**Nuanced Meaning 1**	**Nuanced Meaning 2**
Said	Whispered	Murmured
Read	Peruse	Scrutinize
Walk	Meander	Trudge

Reflection Activities

1. Let's put it into practice! Planning for the nuances of action verbs will enable you to model a more robust vocabulary to your students. Complete the chart that follows with two additional nuanced verbs.

Action Verbs & Nuanced Meanings		
Verb	**Nuanced Verb 1**	**Nuanced Verb 2**
Talk		
Need		
Go		

2. Make a conscious effort to substitute the nuanced verbs in place of the common verbs to provide more precise meaning for your students. Which verbs did you introduce?

____

3. How did you ensure that your students understood the new vocabulary?

____

____

____

____

4. As an experiment, count the number of times you use the word "go" in a day, or call in a peer to observe you. What did you discover?

____

____

____

The word "go" is very general and redundant. In addition, it is a word that is acquired very early on in language learning. Try replacing that word with the more precise alternatives for the word "go" that you brainstormed. Think how your listeners might receive your message differently. They might listen more closely instead of tuning out. They might be able to visualize in order to help them better understand. It would also reduce the potential for communication misunderstandings on the part of a listener. For example, instead of, "We are going to music class," try "We will be walking to music class." While some students might assume walking is intended, others will now know we are not running to music class.

5. How will you ensure that your students have continued exposure to the new vocabulary? What next steps will you take?

____

____

____

____

Praising Students

Offering praise to students is a vital part of our classrooms each day throughout the day. If we are not careful we might be tempted to use the same word or phrase to praise students. For that reason, giving praise to our students is a good place to expand our repertoire of elevated language. Before we look at some alternative phrases, answer the following question.

Reflection Question

1. How do you typically praise your students? Jot down the words or phrases you most often use. ___________________________

____

____

____

2. Here is a list of words and phrases that you could use to praise students. Highlight or circle a few that you would like to start using. Try some new phrases each week!

Well done.	I'm speechless.	Excellent.	Very impressive.
Well Executed.	That's exceptional.	You've mastered it.	I'm impressed.
Outstanding work.	That's noteworthy.	That's stupendous.	You hit the nail on the head.
First-class work.	That's tremendous.	Fantastic.	I couldn't have said it better myself.

Figure 4c.1 Happy/Sad Opposites on a Continuum

Opposites on a Continuum

Opposites on a Continuum is a strategy that Carmen created to introduce new vocabulary. Identify each word you want to teach, for example: the word "miserable." Then consider the most basic, polar-opposite vocabulary words related to "miserable," such as happy and sad. Write these on a continuum. Learners will immediately be able to latch on to the concept of happy and sad, two words very familiar to most students. Once "happy" and "sad" have been anchored at opposite ends of the continuum, add your new word, "miserable" on the continuum near the word that it is closest to in meaning. See Figure 4c.1.

This strategy helps to give students an approximate definition of new vocabulary words. As their knowledge grows, you can add words to the continuum and rearrange the word order. For example, you may decide with your students that "miserable" is a worse state than "sad" and needs to be moved to the right of sad. Additional words could be added, such as "elated" and "ecstatic," as they are encountered in texts or as the need for their use in speech arises. Continuums can be kept in a student's notebook to help them keep track of their language learning.

Opposites on a Continuum for Young Learners

Kelly Adams, a Pre-K ELD coach in an urban district, adapted Carmen's Opposites on a Continuum activity to make it accessible for the youngest budding learners. To do so, she adapted the activity into three parts: (1) explaining the concept of opposites, (2) developing sorts with pairs of polar opposites, and (3) engaging in a read-aloud to reinforce the concept of opposites.

Kelly noted that the concept of opposites needs to be explicitly explained to young learners. Following is the progression that Kelly used, primarily in small groups across multiple classroom visits, to introduce the concept. To do this, Kelly chooses pairs of opposites that are relatable to her young learners, such as:

- day/night
- happy/sad

- big/small
- silly/serious
- full/empty

She introduces these polar opposites using pictures accompanied with word labels. Kelly explains that she carefully chooses pictures that best provide the meaning of the words. For example, a bright light bulb represents light, and a dark room with a candle flickering represents dark. Students explore the pairs of opposites as their teacher supports their comprehension with total physical response, gestures, and voice inflection. For example, students copy their teacher in covering and uncovering their eyes for the words dark and light, gesture with their hands to illustrate big and small, and use voice inflection for the emotions happy and sad. Not only do English learners benefit from these scaffolds, but proficient English speakers do too.

Kelly then played a game with students in small groups using opposites on picture cards. Keeping one card from each pair, Kelly gives the opposite from each set to students. She shows her card and then asks, "Who has the opposite of ________?" This requires that students engage in conversations about the pictures. Students are exposed to multiple repetitions of the targeted vocabulary as they use the words in their own speech and listen to others. As the opposites are identified, they are placed at opposite ends of the

Figure 4c.2 Set up for Opposites on a Continuum Activity

continuum. Figure 4c:2 shows how the game is set up as well as samples of the flash cards.

As a second procedure to reinforce the concept of opposites, she, along with fellow Pre-K coaches Barb Schmid and Trudy Eby also crafted a T-chart that requires the students to sort cards into the correct column. Examples of the picture cards used include items and actions related to the polar opposites. Some cards represent "fast," such as a fast car, a rollercoaster, or a child sliding down a slide, while others represent "slow," such as a snail and a sloth. Trudy noted, "When teachers reuse the same architecture of a lesson, for example the same strategy, format, or visual, the familiarity allows children to focus on the new learning as opposed to the how-to of the lesson" (T. Eby, personal communication, May 15, 2022).

Kelly also carries the concept of opposites into her teaching of literature. One method is while reading picture books, she discusses the emotions the main characters are feeling and plots picture supports of the characters and their emotions along a continuum.

The second method is through an interactive read-aloud of *The Tiny Seed* by Eric Carle. Before reading the story, Kelly prepares students for the new vocabulary by drawing an arrow extending in two directions. This is an adaptation of Carmen's Opposites on a Continuum that can be used to facilitate future conversations centered around adjectives. At one end, she writes the

Figure 4c.3 Read Aloud Graphic for Opposites on a Continuum

word "small" in small letters, and at the other end she writes "BIG" in big letters. As she reads the story, students are introduced to a "tiny" seed. She writes the word "tiny" in small letters closest to the word "small." Throughout the story, students learn that the tiny seed grows into a giant sunflower. This prompts Kelly to add a picture of a giant sunflower, along with the word "GIANT," which she writes in all capital letters close to the word "BIG." See Figure 4c:3 for a graphic of the adaptation.

Reflection Questions

1. Let's give Opposites on a Continuum a try with the opposites "big" and "small."
   a. Anchor the words "big" and "small" on opposite ends of a continuum.
   b. Decide where to add the following new vocabulary words on the continuum: "huge," "immense," "enormous," "colossal," "gargantuan," "miniscule," "infinitesimal," "microscopic," "miniature," "minute."

2. Now let's try the strategy Opposites on a Continuum with the synonyms "old" and "new."
   a. Anchor the words "old" and "new" on opposite ends of a continuum.
   b. Decide where to add the following new vocabulary words on the continuum: "senior," "ancient," "prehistoric," "mature," "elderly," "modern," "current," "neoteric," "latest," "pristine."

Paint Strips and Shades of Meaning

Teaching the shades of meanings of words occurs best when done in context, through experiences when possible. In this way, word meanings are quickly understood by all. Shanahan (2005) emphasized, "The importance of vocabulary is beyond doubt . . . such knowledge is integral to any activities that involve language, and psychologists have shown how vocabulary is more than a list of 'word meanings in the mind,' but actually functions as an index of a much richer and harder to measure constellation of understandings and experiences" (p. 88).

Paint strips, found in any hardware store, are a creative way to aid students' understanding of nuanced meanings of words that are similar. Consider, for example, the meaning of the word "kind" and the three additional words listed beneath. While all four words are positive attributes, each adjective has a slightly nuanced meaning.

Kind = willingness to do good
Considerate = thoughtful of the rights and feelings of others
Generous = a willingness to give to or share with others
Altruistic = showing a selfless concern for the well-being of others

Paint strips are a great way to introduce students to words that have shades of differences in meaning. While the paint strips all have shades of color within the same palate, each one is slightly different. The Common Core State Standards are replete with the phrase "use precise language." In order

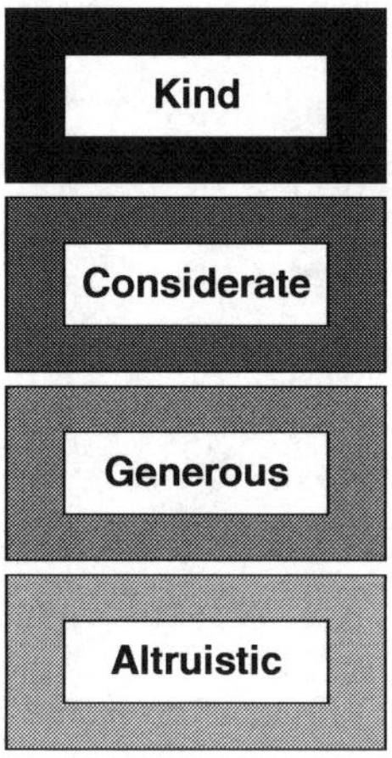

Figure 4c.4 Paint Strip Graphic for Nice

to use precise language, our students need to be exposed to the nuanced meaning of words.

Teachers can aid our students' acquisition of vocabulary by modeling new words appropriately in context in their own speech. For example, if someone holds the door for an individual using crutches, you might say, "Thank you for being considerate of others." When someone gives a pencil to another student in need of one, you could say, "Now that was being generous." Carmen recounts the perfect opportunity she had to commend a student for being altruistic:

> I had made a batch of my famous chocolate chip cookies as a reward for my class. The class had been working extremely hard for this coveted treat. The moment finally arrived when I was passing out the cookies. Everyone quickly devoured the cookies; everyone except for one student. One student left his untouched on the paper napkin. When I asked him why he wasn't eating his cookie, he replied, "I'm saving it for my mom." I knew this student and his mother had fallen on hard times, and my heart was touched by his selfless act. "You, young man, are the most altruistic fifth grader I know. I don't know of many students who would give up their cookie reward so someone else could enjoy it!"

Carmen could have used the phrase, "Wow, that was really nice of you," and her students would have understood the general meaning of the word "nice." However, seizing teachable moments, Carmen was able to introduce nuanced words for "nice" such as "generous," "considerate," and "altruistic." It is important for the teacher to recognize that while these words could fall under the umbrella of "nice," their meanings are slightly different and are often used in different contexts.

A Tribute to Substitutionary Language

As teachers begin their journey of using elevated language, the authors suggest celebrating with their students. Leah Flick, third-grade teacher, noted the following as she began modeling nuanced language in her speech, "My students became more curious about words" (L. Flick, personal communication, May 15, 2022). Leah also observed her students using the words in their speaking and writing. Second-grade teacher, Vicki Stutz noted better listening skills in class since she has implemented the use of sophisticated language in her own speech. "Their listening is better. They're listening for the robust vocabulary." Vicki added, "Students are much more aware of words and ask 'What does that mean?'" (V. Stutz, personal communication, May 15, 2022). Her students have become so intrigued with sophisticated language that they requested she make a chart with fancy college words. Vicki

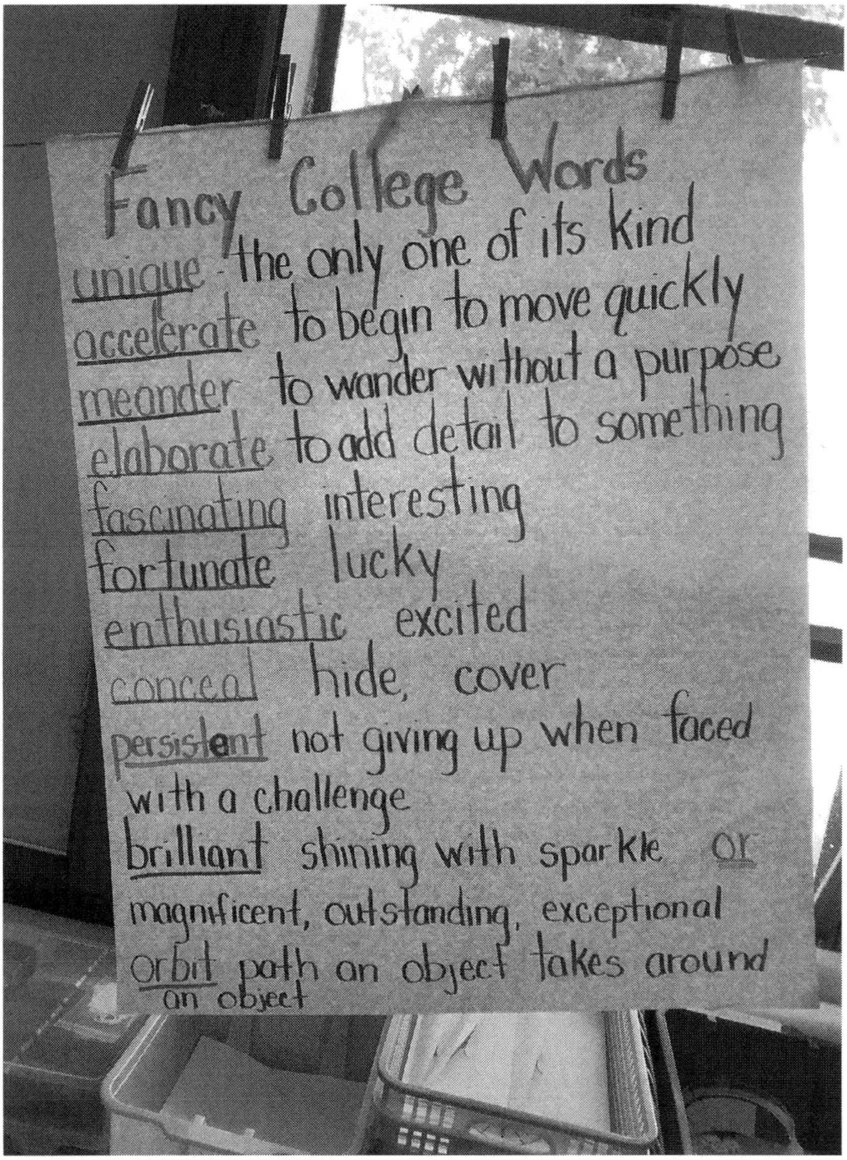

Figure 4c.5 College Words Poster

has started recording new words on a chart that has found a prominent place in the classroom. She noted that her students' momentum for learning new words has not waned, and they are now tracking their own learning. "It's as though they needed permission to use them," she concluded.

Tips for ELs

As ESL teachers, Carmen and Kristen often spend time in their colleagues' classrooms. They often see posters with elevated language or vocabulary on them in the forms of word lists. In the quest for a print-rich classroom, elementary teachers often decorate their walls with posters that may have little practical value for their students. This is especially true in the early childhood and primary classrooms. According to Erika Christakis in her book *The Importance of Being Little: What Preschoolers Really Need From Grownups* (2016), "First we'll bombard you with what educators call a print-rich environment, every wall and surface festooned with a vertiginous array of labels, vocabulary lists, calendars, graphs, classroom rules, alphabet lists, number charts, and inspirational platitudes—few of those symbols you will be able to decode, a favorite buzzword for what used to be known as reading" (p. 33).

Reflection Questions

1. How often do students refer to these types of posters? ____________
   ____
2. What is the pitfall of hanging a poster like this? _________________
   ____

There are many pitfalls to posters such as these. First, some students may not be able to decode the words. Secondly, while they may contain elevated language, they often have no context. As a result, students may not know which words to use when and therefore not reference the posters at all. Unless the teacher has explicitly taught students how to use these posters and the posters are continuously being referenced, they are just another decoration on the wall. Furthermore, depending on where the students sit, they may not be able to easily access the posters' content. What if we could have an easily accessible print-rich environment at our students' fingertips instead of on the walls?

Put It on a Post-it

Fourth-grade and master teacher Allyson Plasterer and ESL teacher Kristen Haase believe students need little more than notebooks and Post-its for their classroom materials. When Allyson and Kristen reach for the Post-its, it is during "in-the-moment teaching." These are "get in and get out" moments, but the students are left with tangible mementos they can keep in their notebooks. When the teachers reach for the Post-its, it sends messages to the students such as "(1) I am going to get information I need at that moment. (2) The information I get at that moment will help me, as an individual, grow as a learner. (3) The teacher cares about me and knows what I need to grow as a learner. (4) I know where to find the information I learned (in my notebook)." And from our experience, the students love collecting Post-its!

As we have said throughout this book, we do not want to add more to teachers' already overfilled plates. We do, however, want teachers to become cognizant of their speech and seize every teachable moment. Some of the most effective learning experiences our students have are when we go off script. Other teachable moments occur when we are one-on-one with students or in a small group. This is when we can hone in on what our students need and meet them where they are at that moment. This provides relevant and timely feedback.

Here are some examples of Post-its you can create on the spot for your students:

- Students ask for substitutionary language—What is a better word for . . .? Consider this conversation between Kristen and one of her former ESL students as they are having a conference:

  Student: Mrs. Haase, what is another word for "sleep"?
  Kristen: Read or tell me the sentence using the word "sleep."
  Student: The boy sleep in the bed.
  Kristen: Got it. Let's talk about some words you could substitute for "sleep." (Haase quickly creates the following chart on a Post-it.)

  Sleep

Light/Short doze, rest, snooze, siesta	Deep/Long slumber, deep sleep, hibernate

  Kristen: Now, substitute one of those words or phrases and say the whole sentence.
  Student: The boy slumber in the bed. (This is also a teachable moment for subject–verb agreement, which is often a challenge for beginning ELs.)
  Kristen: And have you ever heard of a slumber bag?
  Student: No.
  Kristen: What do you think it is?
  Student: I know—it is a place where you can sleep!
  Kristen: Yes (and she sketches a quick visual with the label "slumber bag," which goes in the student's notebook)

- Students can access a visual rather than rely solely on verbal instruction.

  When students were having trouble with the concept of "acceleration," Allyson drew a quick sketch on a Post-it and had her students do the same. This was placed in their science books for future reference.

Figure 4c.6 Put It on a Post-it

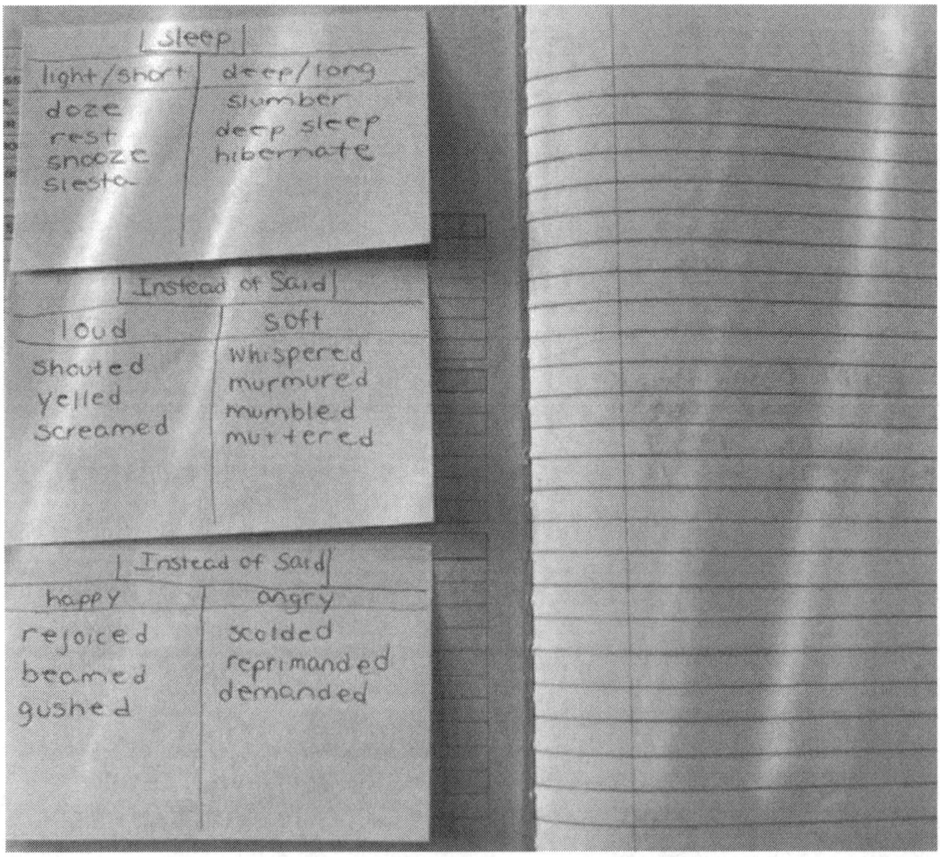

Figure 4c.7 Put It on a Post-it in Student Notebooks

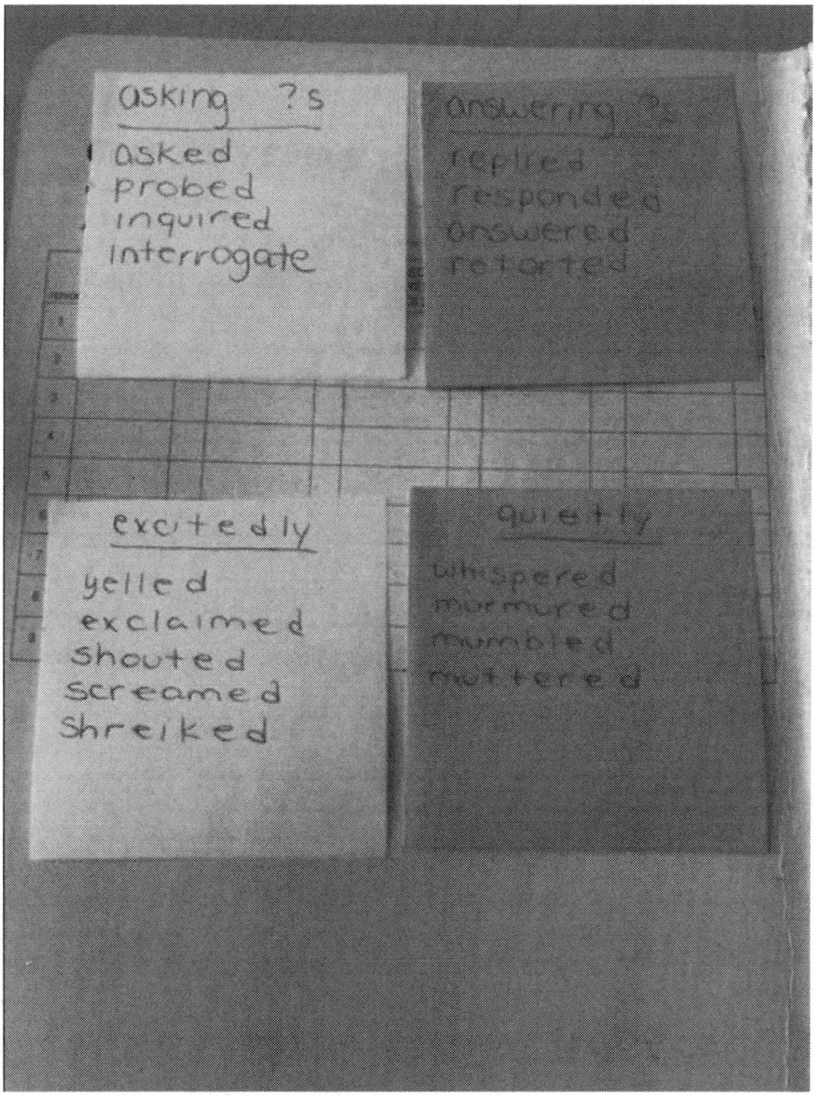

Figure 4c.8 Put It on a Post-it: Words Other Than Said

- Students have their own personal word/picture dictionaries at their disposal.

You might be thinking that this seems very time-consuming. Trust us—it is not. Most teachers spend time conferencing with students one-on-one or in small groups daily. Once it becomes part of your daily routine, it comes naturally and quickly. In addition, it can prevent students from coming up to you and asking the same questions over and over again, because the answer is often in their notebooks on a Post-it. Before the students start working independently, remind them to use their Post-its.

Putting it on a Post-it should become a routine in every teacher's class. By using a visual cue such as a Post-it note, students will be alerted to what comes next: substitutionary language, higher-level vocabulary, and/or a visual of challenging concepts. These Post-its can be stored in a student's notebook or a folder for future reference. Since you have seized on a teachable moment, the individualized lesson has a better chance of sticking because it is customized to the student's individual needs.

References

August, D., & Shanahan, T. (Eds.). (2006). *Executive summary. Developing literacy in second-language learners: Report of the national literacy panel on language-minority children and youth.* Lawrence Erlbaum. www.cal.org/natl-lit-panel/reports/Executive_Summary.pdf

Christakis, E. (2016). *The importance of being little: What preschoolers really need from grownups.* Penguin Publishing.

Shanahan, T. (2005). *The national reading panel report. Practical advice for teachers.* Learning Point Associates/North Central Regional Educational Laboratory (NCREL).

Strategy #4: Using Content Vocabulary Across the Curriculum

Strategy Focus

There are a myriad of opportunities for teachers to use math terms, science terms, and any content-area term outside the classroom. Imagine students hearing these words in the cafeteria, on the playground, in the halls, and during impromptu conversations. Imagine multiple adults within a school setting using these terms with students in different contexts. Teachers will find that as they get into the practice of seizing previous missed opportunities, their students will not only retain those words but also feel empowered to use them.

Strategy #4: Using Content Vocabulary Across the Curriculum

As I am walking down the hall, I try to incorporate math terms into my directions. For example, "Make sure our line is "parallel" to the wall. Now we are going to turn down the next hall so we are "perpendicular" to the last hall. Be sure to stay parallel to the wall." I feel it is important for the students to hear those words in multiple contexts outside the classroom in order for them to understand them.

Lenore Charnock, Third-Grade Teacher
(L. Charnock, personal communication, May 15, 2022)

Introduction

How many times have you said, "I took an advanced math course or science course in high school, but I don't remember any of it"? Or "As soon as I took the test, I forgot the information that was on it." Everyone has uttered those types of comments about one subject or another, but what are some of the reasons? Could it be because we never heard or used the content vocabulary outside of the classroom? Or could it be that the vocabulary words were heard only a handful of times and were not acquired at deeper levels of understanding? Or perhaps once we finished the class or took the test, we no longer had a use for specific content-area vocabulary.

Description of the Strategy

In Chapter 5, we discuss the importance of a schoolwide culture. Imagine students hearing math, social studies, and science terms in the cafeteria, on the playground, in the halls, and during impromptu conversations. Imagine multiple adults within a school setting using these terms with students in different contexts. Teachers will find that as they get into the practice of seizing previous missed opportunities, their students will not only retain those words but also feel empowered to use them.

There are a myriad of opportunities for teachers to use math, social studies, and science terms and any other content-area term outside the classroom. This chapter will give the school staff ideas for using content vocabulary throughout the school day each and every day.

Rationale

What do students need to know? In their article "Increasing Academic Language by Speaking It," Bill and Persida Himmele suggest, "for teachers to increase students' exposure to academic language, it's important that they approach almost any verbal interaction as an opportunity for developing academic language" (Himmele & Himmele, 2009). In order to be successful in content areas, students need to be able to develop a deep understanding of content vocabulary terms. In order for this to occur, there needs to be complete reciprocity with respect to language and vocabulary across the content areas. English language arts teachers need to integrate vocabulary from other subject areas such as math, science, social studies, and the unified arts into their teacher talk. In addition, teachers from those areas need to incorporate academic terms from the literacy classroom in their daily interactions with students.

What's the challenge? From the time children are born until the time they begin school, they are acquiring language and background knowledge through listening and speaking. In their book *Born to Talk*, Hulit et al. (2010) state that children are hardwired for listening and speaking. Reading and writing are optional accessories. Furthermore, Stricht and James (1984) identified a gap between listening and reading comprehension. The ability to access complex ideas requires oral language rather than the written word for most learners until they reach middle school. For some students, the only opportunity for them to be exposed to complex ideas and acquire content vocabulary is in school in content-specific classes.

What does the strategy offer? Stahl (2005) stressed that vocabulary instruction should include repeated exposure in a variety of contexts. In order for students to learn vast amounts of academic vocabulary through repeated exposure, they will need to have many opportunities to hear the vocabulary being used both in the content areas and across the curriculum. The authors understand this is a process. The ideas in this strategy will help educators expose students to challenging content vocabulary throughout the school day.

Carmen likens the process of learning new vocabulary to moving through the concentric circles on a dartboard towards the bullseye. Initially, our job is to get students on the dartboard of meaning. It may start with an approximate meaning, but with each repeated exposure to the word, in a variety of contexts, the meaning of the word becomes clearer; multiple meaning words and their various meanings are understood, and eventually, the student gains confidence to use the word in his or her speaking and writing. This process happens over time, but when exposed to multiple repetitions, the student will eventually reach the bullseye.

The strategy of using elevated vocabulary across content areas provides ample opportunities to model academic vocabulary in a wide variety of contexts and accelerates students' mastery of vocabulary. Carey (1978) found that children may gain a partial understanding of a new word with few exposures, but to fully understand a word and all its meanings most likely takes years and multiple repetitions.

This is one of the reasons it is important for educators to use and reinforce content-area vocabulary outside the content classroom. It goes to

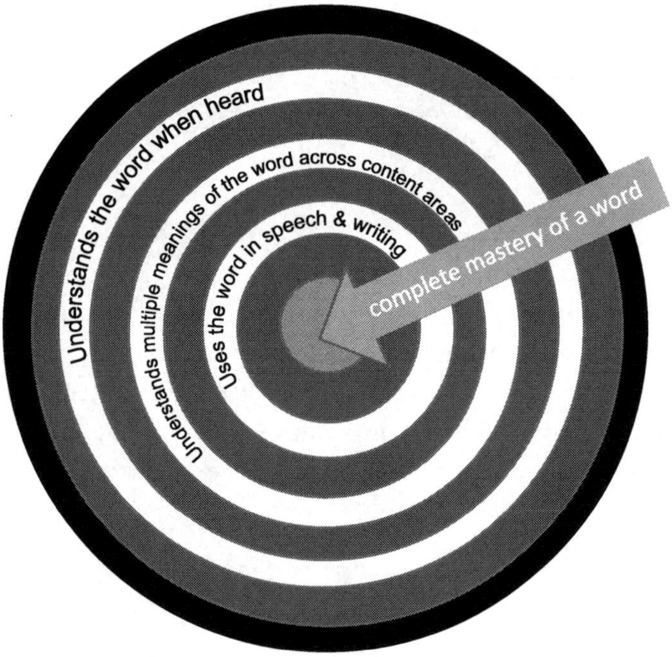

Figure 4d.1 Carmen's Dartboard of Meaning
Source: The Dartboard of Meaning ©2022 Carmen Shahadi Rowe

show that hearing words outside of the content classroom and in different contexts will further help cement the academic words in the students' working vocabulary; thus helping students retain the words in years to come.

The authors emphasize that putting content-area vocabulary words on a word wall is not enough. Putting vocabulary words on word walls has been a long-standing practice. Teachers may teach a word and then place that word on the wall in alphabetical order or keep them up until the unit is over and then replace them. While students may know the words are on the wall, how useful is this to the students? This may look like good optics, but does a word on a wall help the students do more than spell the word correctly?

In addition, many teachers see the importance of pre-teaching math, science, and social studies vocabulary, and we do not discount the importance of doing that. Teachers often do a good job of teaching vocabulary at the word level. However, this is not nearly enough. We need to be modeling correct vocabulary usage at the sentence and the discourse levels. Imagine the impact on the students' content vocabulary if they heard the terminology continuously modeled correctly in context inside and outside of their content classroom.

Ideas in Action

Math

In regard to the math classroom, according to Riccomini et al. (2015), mathematical vocabulary plays an important role in students' language learning which, in turn, has a positive impact on them becoming proficient in the subject area. Seizing opportunities to use math vocabulary outside of the classroom begins with identifying math vocabulary at varying levels. The authors started a chart with grade level, math vocabulary terms.

Grade Level	Numbers and Operations	Algebraic Concepts	Geometry	Measurement and Data
Pre-K and Kindergarten			cone, cube, pattern, sphere	
First Grade	difference	greater than, less than		
Second Grade	Array			length

Grade Level	Numbers and Operations	Algebraic Concepts	Geometry	Measurement and Data
Third Grade	calculate* numerator, denominator, fraction	area perimeter	parallel, perpendicular	inch, centimeter, pictograph, line plot
Fourth Grade			angle, circumference, hypotenuse, diameter	
Fifth Grade	algorithm	brackets coordinate plane		formulas volume

Activity #1: Brainstorm: Opportunities to Use Math Vocabulary Outside of the Math Classroom

In order to use math vocabulary and concepts outside of the classroom, Lenore and Kristen identify a few key terms for each math unit and make a conscious effort to use them outside of the classroom. Here are the steps they take for a geometry unit in which students need to identify, compare, and classify shapes and their attributes:

1. Identify key vocabulary and concepts.

parallel	Perpendicular	quadrilateral

2. Brainstorm situations and locations in which they would use the terms.
   - In the hallway—in the cafeteria
   - On the playground—lining up
3. Create scenarios to use the language in different locations. When Kristen and Lenore first started, they used this chart to guide them.

Put-It-Into-Practice Activity

1. Now it is your turn. Think of a few challenging math terms or concepts. Here are some words/concepts to consider:
   - Multiple meaning words
   - Challenging vocabulary that will most likely not be heard outside the content classroom
   - Challenging concepts that students will need to experience in multiple contexts

Location	Terms/ Concepts	Teachable Moment	Rationale
In the hallway	**quadrilateral**	Have students identify as many examples and different types of **quadrilaterals** as they can. Make a list when they return to the classroom.	While **quadrilaterals** are introduced in elementary school, they are used extensively in theorems in secondary math. Having an understanding of **quadrilaterals** will provide students with a solid foundation.
In the cafeteria	**parallel**	Use the term when assigning seats. "Sit in a seat that is directly across from and **parallel** with your friend."	Using specific directional prepositional phrases with math terms will help students remember because they will have heard them used in a meaningful context outside the classroom. Students will remember the interaction in which you used the term and be able to apply it to their learning in the content classroom.
On the playground	**parallel and perpendicular**	As students are lining up from recess, tell them to form a line **parallel** to the west side of the building and **perpendicular** to the south side of the building.	Using elevated language in a context builds vocabulary without needing to explicitly teach it.

Math Vocabulary/Concepts

1.	2.	3.

After you have chosen 3 math terms or concepts, think of different locations you could use these terms and complete the chart below.

Location	Term or Concept	Teachable Moment	Rationale

Activity #2: Multiple-Meaning Words Often Heard During Math Instruction

Write the first words that come to your mind when you hear these words:

Find ______________________________

Long ______________________________

Table ______________________________

Quarter ______________________________

Now, consider the following . . .

- **Find**—What does it mean? While in some cases, "find" may mean to locate, in math terminology, it also may mean you need to calculate.
- **Long**—The most literal meaning may refer to the length of an object, but it can also refer to elapsed time.
- **Table**—Most students know a table for eating but get confused when they see it used as a chart.
- **Quarter**—This word could refer to money, time, or parts and wholes during a fraction unit. For example, we may say, "quarter the apple," meaning I am going to cut it into four pieces.

Social Studies

Timelines

Social studies content is replete with names of specific people, places, events, and concepts.

Background knowledge presents itself as a challenge for many students. Students are expected not only to become familiar with the key people, places, events, and concepts but also to understand cause-and-effect relationships within this content area. When the academic vocabulary is presented to students as a once-and-done lesson, students are often left unsure about the overarching themes and connections to their world and the people and events that impacted change. Using timelines in the classroom is an effective way to ensure that teachers and students alike have access to the key vocabulary during the teaching of social studies.

Understanding chronology, or the order in which events occurred, is important in aiding our understanding of history. The timeline in what follows is a portable timeline Carmen created and used with her students while

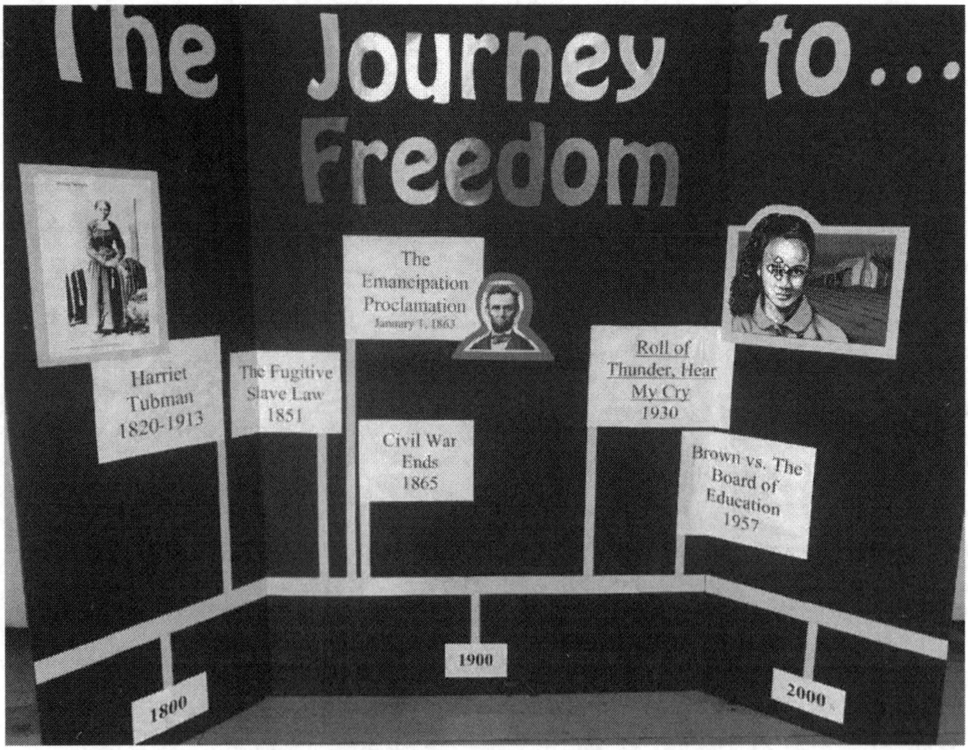

Figure 4d.2 Journey to Freedom Timeline

teaching a unit on slavery in the United States. The timeline made available the term "emancipation proclamation" as well as the name "Abraham Lincoln," the president who issued the proclamation. Carmen and her students referred to the timeline daily during their class discussions. The timeline initiated the following question from one of her former fifth-grade students: "If President Lincoln signed the Emancipation Proclamation in 1863, why did the Civil War not end until 1865?" Carmen doubts this question would have been asked, using the names of events and key individuals, without the visual aid of the timeline. In this case, the chronology of events was made accessible through the use of a timeline. Carmen emphasized, "The timeline served as a reminder to my students and myself to use the key terms and vocabulary of the content we were studying."

During a math lesson, Lenore and Kristen decided to use social studies terms around voting in a content area in which they are not typically used. For this activity they chose the words "poll," "vote," "ballot," and "tally." Notice that the definitions have remained the same, but the context has changed to provide students with additional exposures to the words. This strategic modeling will increase the likelihood that the students will retain the meanings of the words.

Social Studies Word or Phrase	Using the Words and Phrases in the Math Classroom
Poll	Today, we are going to take a <u>poll</u> of our class.
Vote	We are going to <u>vote</u> on our favorite color.
Ballot	We are going to write our choice on a piece of paper and place it in the <u>ballot</u> box.
Tally	We will get the poll results by <u>tallying</u> the votes that were placed in the ballot box.

Put-It-Into-Practice Activity

1. Generate a list of vocabulary terms or phrases that you use in a unit of study. These words and phrases may come from social studies or another content area. As you generate the list, brainstorm times when you could use these words outside of their normal content area.

______________ (Content Area) Word or Phrase	Using the Words and Phrases in the ______________ (Different Than the First Column) Content Classroom

Science

Think of how often you use science vocabulary in everyday conversation. Think of how many index cards were made for learning science vocabulary and terms. Did you retain any of those terms after the test? What if we were to infuse science vocabulary across the curriculum?

According to music teacher Matt Pavelko, there are many opportunities to use elevated language in the music classroom. In the simplest of examples, using the vocabulary word "duration" and defining it in connection with other terms such as "endurance" that reinforce the understanding of the word, it is possible to make connections to high-level vocabulary across multiple contexts. Matt states, "The inherent nature of music to connect with other subjects provides a tremendous platform for intentionally employing vocabulary to expand students' use of more advanced language"(M. Pavelko, personal communication, May 15, 2022).

In one example, Matt discusses a unit about the science of sounds that includes vocabulary in reference to sound waves. The terms "amplitude," "frequency," "intensity," "decibel," "vibration," "pitch," and "volume" are all used in scientifically accurate ways to define the nature and behavior of sound waves. During this unit, students experience sound waves as vibration with their eyes, ears, and hands. With Matt's guidance, students are able to connect the vocabulary words "amplitude," "intensity," and "volume" in a way that is both relevant to fourth- and-fifth grade students and scientifically accurate and applicable in other settings. For example, they discuss light waves, ocean waves, and barometric pressure waves in weather systems. By using terms in his lessons in the music classroom that students need to know in the science classroom, Matt is able to expose students to language that is often not heard outside the content classroom.

In Chapter 5, we discussed the importance of creating a schoolwide culture of bolstering students' language by having all staff model elevated language. In order to do this, staff across grade levels and specialized areas must seize on opportunities to plan together. Matt speaks with intermediate teachers in order to generate a list of scientific terms that students need to know in order to be successful in the classroom.

Put-It-Into-Practice Activity

Following is an example of words heard in the music classroom as well as in the science classroom. Depending on the context, the words may have similar meanings or completely different meanings. Complete the third column of the chart by finding additional uses of the musical terms in the science classroom and beyond.

Music Word or Phrase	Using the Words and Phrases in the Music Classroom	Using the Words and Phrases in the Science Classroom and Beyond
volume	the degree of loudness	• Measure the volume of the liquid in the cylinder. • Let's turn the volume of your voices down.
intensity	the intensity of the music is loud or soft depending on the theme	
Pitch	the degree of highness or lowness of a tone	
frequency	the number of wave cycles in 1 second	

Tips for ELs

Many ESL teachers believe in the importance of pre-teaching vocabulary. If this is modeled correctly, it can be effective. However, as an ESL teacher who has taught third- through fifth grade-math, Kristen rarely pre-teaches vocabulary. Making the connection between pre-teaching vocabulary and the classroom teacher's lesson can be difficult for students. To get the most bang for her buck, Kristen provides on-the-spot vocabulary teaching. Here is an example of how she modeled teacher talk using gesturing and visuals during a lesson on fractions. The vocabulary terms of the lesson are "numerator" and "denominator."

> **Haase**: What is this? (Shows a candy bar). It is one whole candy bar. Do you notice the candy bar is divided into pieces or parts? How many parts do you see? (12 pieces). Watch how I write this as a fraction. (12/12). The top number is the numerator and the bottom number is the denominator. Now I am going to distribute parts of the candy bar to you. Remember how many pieces we started with (12). 12 will be our denominator. The number of pieces you get will be your numerator. I have 2 pieces, so my numerator is 2 and my denominator is 12. What is your numerator and your denominator? Start your answer with "My numerator is __________ and my denominator is __________."

Notice how Kristen did not pre-teach "numerator" and "denominator" but rather incorporated the terms into her lesson. The students received multiple exposures to the academic terms from both the teacher and the other students.

Social studies can be challenging for ELs because of the vast amounts of background knowledge to be learned. In addition, much of the vocabulary represents concepts and may be difficult to teach with a single visual or word substitution. Take, for example, the Revolutionary War. In order to build background knowledge, Carmen narrated sections of the events leading up to the war, complete with props, as students acted out the scenes. Kristen made the Civil Rights Act come to life for her students by recreating scenarios Blacks encountered during the civil rights era. In both of these instances, English Learners became familiarized with the people, places, events, and key concepts essential to their overall understanding of those two events in history through strategic modeling through teacher talk of key concepts. Through these "skits," narrated by the teacher, all students were given the big picture of a particular slice of history being studied and, in the process, gained important background knowledge.

Flip Books

During the reenactment of the early history leading up to the Revolutionary War, Carmen created flip books for her students as a way to help them record key information during their study of history. Each tab of the flip book provided a category of this time period. In this way, as Carmen modeled the key vocabulary in her speech during discussions, students also had a way to access the terms themselves during discussions and later when they were required to write an essay on the causes of the Revolutionary War.

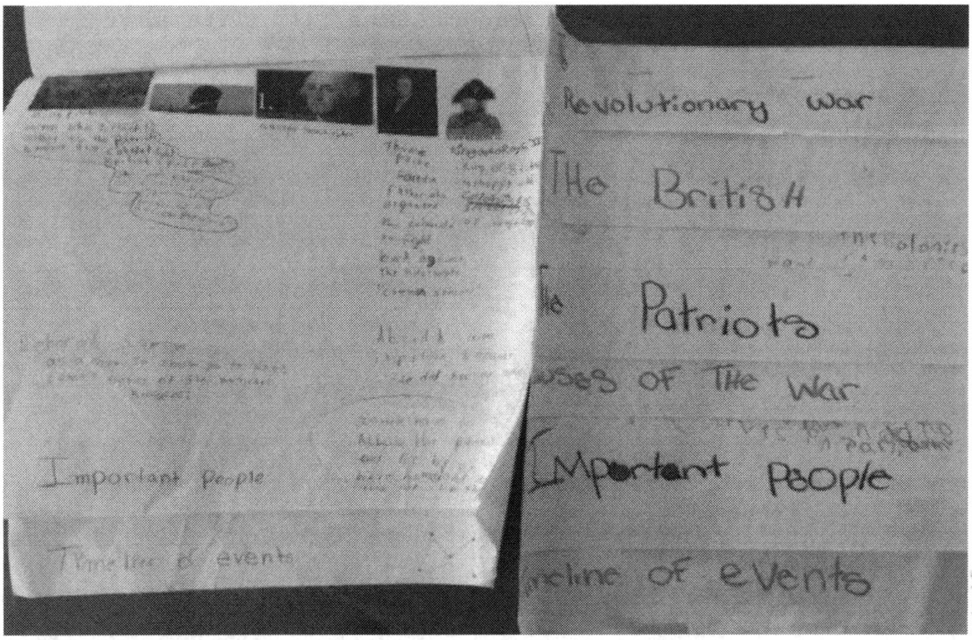

Figure 4d.3 Revolutionary War Flip Book

Before beginning a unit of study, teachers can identify key terms they wish to model in their speech, repeatedly, in order to give their students the "big picture of the social studies unit." Notice in the chart that follow that the key people, place, events, and concepts of the targeted historical eras were all recorded to insure strategic modeling on behalf of the teacher. The third row in the chart has been left blank for you to practice identifying targeted vocabulary of an era in history that you cover with your students.

Era in History	People	Places	Events	Concepts
Revolutionary War	Red Coats, Yankees, King George III, Thomas Paine	England, Boston,	Boston Tea Party, Boston Massacre, speech by King George the III	taxation without representation
Civil Rights Movement	Blacks, Klu Klux Klan, Rosa Parks, Martin Luther King	Alabama, Mississippi, the Southern states	Montgomery bus boycott, civil rights marches	segregation, boycott, separate but equal

The 30-Word Core Content Vocabulary Lists organize vocabulary by content area and grade level and can be useful tools for teachers. Each list contains the top 30 most essential academic vocabulary words needed to meet the rigorous academic standards for that particular content area.

Marzano's 30-Word Core Content Vocabulary Lists

References

Carey, S. (1978). The child as word learner. In M. Halle, J. Bresnan, & G. Miller (Eds.), *Linguistic theory and psychological reality* (pp. 264–293). MIT Press.

Himmele, W., & Himmele, P. (2009). *Increasing exposure to academic language by speaking it*. ASCD.

Hulit, L. M., Howard, M. R., & Fahey, K. R. (2010). *Born to talk: An introduction to speech and language development*. Pearson.

Marzano, R. Vocabulary lists by grade level for LA, Science, SS, and Math

Riccomini, P. J., Smith, G. W., Hughes, E. M., & Fries, K. M. (2015). *The language of mathematics: The importance of teaching and learning mathematical vocabulary* (pp. 235–252). https://doi.org/10.1080/1057

Stahl, S. (2005). Four problems with reteaching word meanings (and what to do to make vocabulary an integral part of instruction). In E. H. Hiebert & M. L. Kamil (Eds.), *Teaching and learning vocabulary: Bringing research to practice* (pp. 95–114). Lawrence Erlbaum.

Stricht, T. G., & James, J. H. (1984). Listening and reading. In P. D. Pearson, R. Barr, M. L. Kamil, & P. Mosenthal (Eds.), *Handbook of reading research* (Vol. 1, pp. 293–317). Longman.

Strategy #5: Getting Your Morning Started Right

Strategy Focus

Capitalizing on predictable and inevitable encounters that occur in the morning as students begin their day is a great place to model elevated language. In this chapter, the authors present various scenarios and routines, typically presented in the morning, as opportunities in which to help students get their day started on the right note by exposing them to rich language.

Strategy #5: Getting Your Morning Started Right

Introduction

Morning routines are an integral part of the school day. Students are greeted at the entrance of the school, as they walk through the halls, and as they enter their classrooms. Students may encounter multiple staff members before they even sit down to start their day. Teachers often give instructions to the students as they come in, or the instructions are displayed on the board. Morning announcements are another part of the morning routine. In addition, most elementary teachers and students start their day by having a morning meeting. What if, during these predictable and inevitable encounters, school staff used elevated language during all of these scenarios? What if substitutionary language was used to replace some of the common words and phrases modeled by staff?

Description

As part of the schoolwide culture discussed in Chapter 5, the authors suggest all staff model elevated language in their interactions with students. In addition, staff members would eliminate common, everyday words and phrases and replace them with academic vocabulary and elevated language. Furthermore, the staff would not repeat the same academic vocabulary and elevated language. They would "mix it up" from time to time.

Rationale

A common thread throughout our book is the need for students to have multiple exposures to elevated language throughout their day in order to bolster their vocabularies. We also know common words and phrases are heard a myriad of times throughout the career of an elementary student. Phrases and questions like "Good morning, class" and "How are you?" are heard continuously throughout a students' tenure.

Academic language proficiency is widely recognized as a pivotal factor in the school success of English learners, and it has been cited as a major contributor to achievement gaps between language-minority students and English-proficient students (Francis et al., 2006). While this research pertains to English language learners, the authors contend that this applies to all students. We refer again to Stahl (2005), who emphasized that all students need opportunities to be exposed to robust vocabulary repeatedly and in many contexts. If we are to bolster our students' language, we need to use an academic register in the classroom by seizing every possible opportunity to expand our students' vocabularies by modeling elevated language. Morning routines are a great opportunity to model language that students may encounter in literature and academic texts. Furthermore, when staff members' language becomes predictable, students tend to tune them out. Thus, we have missed an opportunity to expose our students to new and fresh language that has the potential to help them succeed in the academic classroom.

Ideas in Action

Since Kristen is not a classroom teacher, she serves on outdoor duty at the beginning and end of each day. She always seizes this opportunity to use elevated language. Here are some examples of the way she greets the students when they come in the door:

Instead of . . .	Replace With . . .
Good morning.	Greetings. Salutations. Top of the morning to you. Welcome.
Good to see you.	Pleasure to see you. Grateful you are here. Splendid to see you. Pleased by your timely arrival.
How are you?	How is the world treating you? What is new with you? What's the latest buzz in your world?
Hope you have a good day.	Hope you have a productive day. Wishing you a pleasant day.

Reflection Activity

When you greet your students individually in the morning, what words or phrases could you substitute for more common ones? Choose a few from the list given, or create your own and write them below. Make a point to use them each morning. Note your students' reaction!

____

____

____

On the Morning Announcements

The morning announcements are a prime time to interject elevated language and academic vocabulary into the students' day. The authors' position is that strategic modeling occurs best when it is done in authentic ways across the school day, including during the morning announcements. We also suggest the students use elevated language if they are delivering the announcements. In this way, students learn that not only teachers serve as role models of elevated languages, but they can, too.

Remember when we discussed the importance of using content across the curriculum? The morning announcements provide an opportunity to do so. For example, while telling your captive audience about the weather, substitute content vocabulary from science for common weather terms. What is one way to do this? Adding adjectives is a simple way to elevate an ordinary phrase. While we may use adjectives of color, number, and size in everyday speech, more descriptive adjectives used in literature and academic texts are less frequently used in social language. It is important to note: Students hear and will continue to hear these common phrases thousands of times over the course of their lives. Why not build on these phrases? Let's look at how we can do this with weather terms.

Describing the Weather

Common Phrases	Add Adjectives . . .	Or Substitute . . .
It is sunny.	It is a brilliant, sunny day.	It is a sunlit day.
It is cloudy.	The sky is darkened on this cloudy day.	The sky is overcast and dreary.

Using adjectives to describe weather and other nouns serves multiple purposes:

Descriptive adjectives . . .

1. make the content more interesting, thereby increasing student engagement
2. allow listeners to create more precise visuals in their minds
3. enable the speaker to build on the background knowledge of the student
4. provide students with the vocabulary they will encounter in academic text, thereby boosting their ability to comprehend the written word

Put-It-Into-Practice Activity

1. Now it is your turn. Think of some common weather terms. Complete the following chart using substitutionary and elevated language. Be sure to use at least one or two adjectives when describing the weather. The following features of weather may help: sunshine, cloudiness, humidity, precipitation, temperature, wind, and visibility. Remember to use a variety of words from week to week!

Common Phrases	Add Adjectives . . .	Or Substitute . . .

To further bolster your students' vocabulary and knowledge, take your description of the weather a step farther. If there are clouds in the sky that day, mention what type of clouds. This helps students:

- acquire the precise names of different clouds, which is part of the science curriculum
- recognize what type of weather is associated with each type of cloud
- predict the weather based on the type of clouds they see in the sky
- sound like meteorologists as they use the content vocabulary in their speech and writing

After they become familiar with the different types of clouds, they will be able to take that knowledge with them and discuss it with their families outside the school walls. We predict your students will look up upon leaving school each and every day!

Examples:

- It is going to be a bright, sunny day. I know this because I noticed puffy, cottony, cumulus clouds in the sky this morning.
- There is a solid chance of thunderstorms today. I know this because I observed dense, dark cumulonimbus clouds in the sky this morning.

***A caution to consider about morning announcements:

Having a word of the week on the morning announcements is a form of explicit teaching, while using substitutionary language is a form of implicit teaching. While introducing a word of the day or week has the potential to build vocabulary, most likely the words would need to be heard multiple times and in different contexts, not just on the morning announcements. We believe that teaching vocabulary in isolation and over a short period of time does not have the same staying power as does using it repeatedly over time in different contexts.

Giving Instructions and Morning Work

After greeting students at the door, teachers can direct their students to the whiteboard. On the whiteboard, students can find instructions for morning work. In this example of a morning message, Kristen seizes opportunities to model elevated language for her students.

Greetings Researchers,
(salutation) (Profession)

After unpacking your personal belongings and storing your items in the closet, return
(adjective) (action verb phrase)
promptly to your workspace. After you have set your intention for the day, commence with your
(adverb) (verb)
morning work immediately. You will locate your morning work following this message.
(adverb) (verb)

Warmly,
(closing)
Mrs. Haase

While a message laden with robust language, such as the one shown, may not be written on the first day of school, over time, with the consistent use of substitutionary language, students will understand the rich vocabulary modeled by teachers not only in their speech but also in their writing.

Put-It-Into-Practice Activity

1. Using Kristen's message as a template, fill in the blanks in this "Mad Lib" with words you would use to create an example of a morning message that you could use with your students.

_______________ _______________
(salutation) (profession)
After unpacking your _______________ belongings and _______________, return
(adjective) (action verb phrase)
_______________ *to your workspace. After you have set your intention for*
(adverb)
the day, _______________ with yourmorning work _______________.
(verb) (adverb)
You will _______________ your morning work following this message.
(verb)

_______________,
(closing)
Mrs. Haase

Classroom Occupations in the Content Areas

Here are some examples of how teachers can refer to their students in the content-area classroom:

Content Area	Professions
English Language Arts	poet, author, journalist, anchorperson, scriptwriter
Science	botanist, chemist, ecologist, astronomer, zoologist, geographer, cytologist (study of cells), meteorologist, researcher
Math	technologist, mathematician, statistician
Social Studies	historian, sociologist, lobbyist, politician

Content Area	Professions
Music	musician, cellist, violinist, soloist, recording engineer, composer
Art	artist, painter, sculptor, Impressionist, illustrator, animator, graphic designer, photographer
Physical Education & Health	athlete, nutritionist, personal trainer, dietician, sports commentator, statistician, coach

Reflection Activity

2. Can you think of other opportunities to use more precise, elevated language in regard to classroom professions? Add your ideas to the chart.
3. Which of the classroom professions are appropriate for the content you teach? Write those here and plan to model these in your speech on a regular basis.

____

____

____

As teachers begin utilizing occupations in their teacher talk, the authors suggest seizing the opportunity to do an "on-the-spot" lesson about suffixes. In addition, modeling other words in the same word family (see Strategy #9) lends itself nicely as follow-up modeling when students have repeatedly been exposed to the root words in the occupations. For example: During a seed-planting activity, Carmen used the following, "My, what fine botanists we have. You are caring for your plants so well. You not only enjoy working with plants but also love reading about botany." Then, as students' plants began to grow, she added another word from the same family: "My botanists have done such a good job with their plants. It's starting to look like a botanical garden in here!"

During Morning Meeting

Morning meetings and routines are a way that teachers can address listening and speaking standards. They also allow opportunities for students to build on their background knowledge.

Morning meeting is always an excellent time to revisit some of the information from the morning announcements. If teachers are able to use some of the same language from the morning announcements in their morning meetings, the likelihood of the students remembering the language increases. A common message of this book is the importance of hearing elevated discourse throughout the day. Morning meetings are a prime time to capitalize on building your students' language and vocabulary.

Tips for ELs

During the morning meeting is an opportunity for ELs to develop social and academic language. It is a time in which they can interact with their English-speaking peers. However, depending on the proficiency level of the EL, morning meetings can deliver information overload. This is why it is important for the teacher to consider different strategies to deliver the message.

Directions of the Day

Oftentimes, classroom teachers comment that ELs have difficulty following directions. To help alleviate this problem, Janet Purcell wrote a simple curriculum called "Directions of the Day." It can be done in an oral or written format. The oral version is preferable for beginning-level Els, and the written version is more helpful to upper-level ELs. Directions of the Day is a convenient and consistent way to begin every class. It usually takes less than 5 minutes to complete the task. When students first enter the room, they should each be ready with a clean sheet of notebook paper. Each day, after the students have completed their directions, have them place their papers on your desk so that there will be no "answer editing."

The teacher will give oral or post written directions, which will become more and more difficult as the students' progress. One set of directions is given per day. An example of directions for the first 10 days is listed in what follows. The directions can be used both orally and in a written format.

Oral Directions of the Day

As noted before, the oral directions are more appropriate for beginning English learners. It is similar to TPR (total physical response). When the students enter the room, they should each be ready with a clean sheet of notebook paper. The teacher will give oral directions, which will become more and more difficult as the students' progress. Following is a chart to refer to before giving oral directions to beginning-level students.

Dos	Don'ts
Speak clearly and pause after phrases or individual directions.	Use slang or idiomatic language.
Repeat directions in the exact same way every time.	Make side comments that will distract the students' listening.
Repeat directions as often as students request.	Speak so slowly that you distort the correct pronunciation of the words.
Use gestures and visuals if possible.	React negatively when you have to repeat too often.
Have students follow directions immediately after they are given.	Force entering and beginning ELs to speak before they are ready.
Teach students to "whisper-repeat" directions to themselves to improve memory.	Be afraid to model the response to the direction if necessary.

Written Directions of the Day

For higher-level students, I have found that the written directions were more transferable to classroom usage as a test strategy. It is very convenient to type the directions in a large font and post them on the board so that the students can immediately begin when they enter the room. Each day, after the students have completed their directions, have them place their papers on your desk so that there will be no "answer editing."

How to Score the Answers

After each simple activity, have the students put their sheets on the board with a magnet or on a bulletin board so that all can see all the answer sheets. As a group, look at each sheet and decide if that student followed the directions exactly as stated or not. Then score each sheet with either a happy face or a sad face. These scores can later easily be tallied for grading purposes.

Sample Directions

Below are suggestions of directions for the first 10 days of class.

Day 1: Write your first and last names on the paper. Underline your last name.

Day 2: Write the number 2 in the top left corner of your paper. Write your initials on the top right corner of your paper.

Day 3: From now on, write the number of the direction in the top left corner. So today, write number 3 in the top left corner. Starting today, always write your initials in the top right corner of your paper. Now write two sentences about an animal you like.

Day 4: Write your initials and the number 4 in the correct place on your paper. Write your first name and your last name on the first line of the paper. On the second line, write the first six letters of the alphabet.

Day 5: Write your initials and the number in the correct place on your paper. On the first line of the paper, write the first letter of your first name and your last name. Skip a line. On the next line, write the even numbers from 1 to 8.

Day 6: Write your initials and the number 6 in the correct place on your paper. On the front of your paper, write your first name backward. On the back side of the paper, write your age.

Day 7: Write your initials and the number 7 in the correct place on your paper. On the front of your paper, write your last name. On the back side of the paper, write your birthday.

Day 8: Write your initials and the number 8 in the correct place on your paper. On the front of your paper, draw two circles. Draw one circle below the other. Write your last name in the higher circle and your first name in the lower circle.

Day 9: Write your initials and the number 9 in the correct place on your paper. Draw two circles next to each other on your paper. Write your teacher's last name in the circle on the left and write your last name in the circle on the right.

Day 10: Write your initials and the number 10 in the correct place on your paper. Fold your paper vertically. Open up the fold and write your home address on the left side. Write the name of the student next to you on the right side.

Writing Your Own Directions

If students seem to have difficulty correctly following the directions of a new concept (i.e., fold the paper horizontally or vertically), carefully discuss what the correct response to the directions would be. The next day, add another direction that includes the confusing one and see if they now can correctly respond.

Some suggested new concepts that could be included are:

- number the lines
- skip a line

- front of the paper
- back of the paper
- fold horizontally (hamburger style)
- fold vertically (hot dog style)
- outline or trace (a pencil, your hand)
- fold in quarters, eighths
- write backward
- put in alphabetical order
- write parents' names
- write your address
- write your phone number
- write your mom's/dad's cell phone number
- write your city, state, zip code
- write specific numbers
- write odd, even numbers
- write addition/subtraction/multiplication/division problem
- write specific shapes in specific places (circle, oval, pyramid, diamond)
- draw shapes within shapes
- write specific information about the students (i.e., boys, girls, wearing blue, wearing long sleeves, hair color, etc.)
- write a sentence with more than six words about a specific topic.
- draw an imaginary animal and write a specific number of sentences about it
- utilizing a map of the United States, include a map key or directional instructions: north, south, east, west, northeast, northwest, etc. Ask about locations of states, i.e., Which state is between New York and Maryland?

References

Francis, D., Rivera, M., Lesaux, N., Kieffer, M., & Rivera, H. (2006). *Practical guidelines for the education of English language learners: Research-based recommendations for instruction and academic interventions*. RMC Research Corporation, Center on Instruction.

Stahl, S. (2005). Four problems with reteaching word meanings (and what to do to make vocabulary an integral part of instruction). In E. H. Hiebert & M. L. Kamil (Eds.), *Teaching and learning vocabulary: Bringing research to practice* (pp. 95–114). Lawrence Erlbaum.

Strategy #6: Using Multiple Meaning Words Across Content Areas

Strategy Focus

This chapter will explore strategies for how content-area teachers can help students recognize words that have different meanings across content areas. For example, most students may know one or two definitions of the word "scale" but don't realize it has other meanings depending on the context. The reader will not only become familiar with common multiple meaning words but also gain strategies for introducing them to their students.

Strategy #6: Using Multiple Meaning Words Across Content Areas

Introduction

Multiple meaning words are words with one or more meanings that change in different contexts. When students hear a multiple meaning word, they must quickly assess the correct meaning of the word from its many possible meanings in that particular context. Multiple meaning words are prevalent in the English language. The following sentences display the multiple meanings of the word "draft":

- We may feel a *draft* of air from a window left open.
- During wartime, a *draft* may be instituted.
- Young men are *drafted* into the armed forces.
- When in school, we will inevitably be asked to hand in a *draft* of an essay for preliminary feedback from the teacher.

Description

This strategy involves exposing students to multiple meaning words in a variety of contexts so that they are able to learn additional meanings of words.

Rationale

What do students need to know? "Key to students' vocabulary development is building rich and flexible word knowledge" (CCSS, p. 32). This vocabulary development happens through repeated exposure to vocabulary across content areas. Students must be able to distinguish the meaning of words in a context in order to comprehend the speaker's and the writer's intention.

What's the challenge? According to a study by Parent (2012), "for most of the homonyms (see definition below), the most common meaning accounts for 90% or more of the total use of the form" (p. 69). For example, the percentage for using the word "hide" meaning "to conceal" is 98.6%, while the other meaning, "skin," is used only 1.4% of the time. Consequently, learners do not recognize that the word "hide" has a different meaning in addition to "to conceal" when they hear or read it in the text. Students often learn the most common and concrete meaning of a word.

What does the strategy offer? Our job is to help students gain an awareness that many words in the English language have more than one meaning. This awareness, coupled with teachers who deliberately use multiple meaning words in a variety of contexts, helps to accelerate the acquisition of vocabulary. In turn, teaching multiple meaning words helps students develop a robust vocabulary. As they increase their knowledge of new meanings of words, they will also increase their listening and reading comprehension.

Before we dive into the strategies, let's identify the categories of multiple meaning words:

1. ***Homophones:*** words that sound the same but are spelled differently and have different meanings. For example: "son" and "sun."
2. ***Homonyms:*** words that sound the same, are spelled the same, but have different meanings. For example, the tickets were invalid. The invalid stayed in his home for weeks.
3. ***Homographs:*** words that sound different, are spelled the same, but have different meanings. They went bass fishing. They sing bass in the choir.

Ideas in Action

One of the most effective ways in which to teach new vocabulary words is in context. This is especially true of multiple meaning words. Carmen recounts the following story . . .

> We were keeping our grandsons for the weekend, Tommy and Jack, almost four and five, respectively. Thanks to our local library, we were well stocked with books and a science kit on electric circuits. As we worked through creating the circuits illustrated in the how-to booklet, I repeated the vocabulary words of each labeled part frequently, as the boys are not yet readers. During our hour-long science experiment, the boys heard scores of repetitions of each word associated with electric circuits. It occurred to me that many of these words our grandsons already knew but in a different context. The chart that follows illustrates their exposure to new vocabulary.

Vocabulary Word	The Context in Which the Word Was Already Understood	The New Context in Which the Words Were Being Used
conductor	The conductor thanked Thomas the Engine.	The wire is our conductor.
switch	All right, boys, let's switch the TV channel.	Look! When we turn the switch on, the light bulb lights up.
power	The Jedi have a lot of power.	The battery is our power source.
closed	I closed the door.	We made a closed circuit, and the light bulb lit up.
open	Open the door.	When we open the circuit, we stop the flow of electricity.

While Tommy and Jack already understood the most concrete meaning of the words listed, they gained exposure to additional meanings of these words that are much more abstract. When Carmen questioned the boys, "Can you open the circuit?" or "Can you make a closed circuit?" they were able to demonstrate that they understood the new meanings of these words. By the end of the time experimenting with circuits, her grandsons had heard the new vocabulary words used scores of times in a new context and even began to use several of the words appropriately in their own speech. She witnessed her grandson, Tommy, declare, "I made a closed circuit!"

Clouds of Meaning

Students typically understand the most literal, concrete meaning of a word first. As teachers introduce additional meanings of the word, it is helpful for students to make the association of various definitions for the same word. Take, for example, the word, "seal." Students can easily grasp the meaning of the animal noun form of the word, our seafaring friend.

But how do we introduce the concept of multiple meaning words to students? In the example, using the noun "seal," we find at least two other meanings for the word in addition to the sea animal: to close, as in to "seal" the envelope, and a "seal" that affirms something is official.

The "clouds of meaning" routine gives students a visual representation and understanding that the same word often has more than one

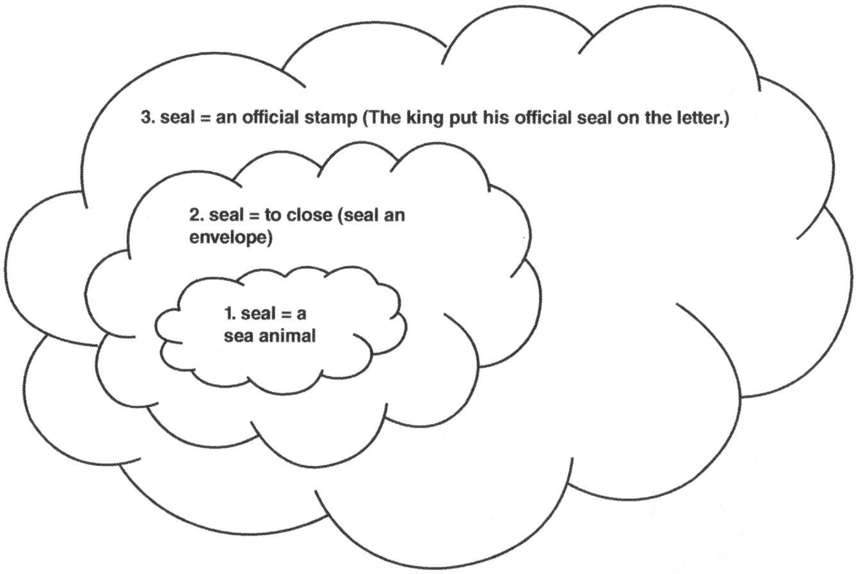

Figure 4f.1 Clouds of Understanding With Text

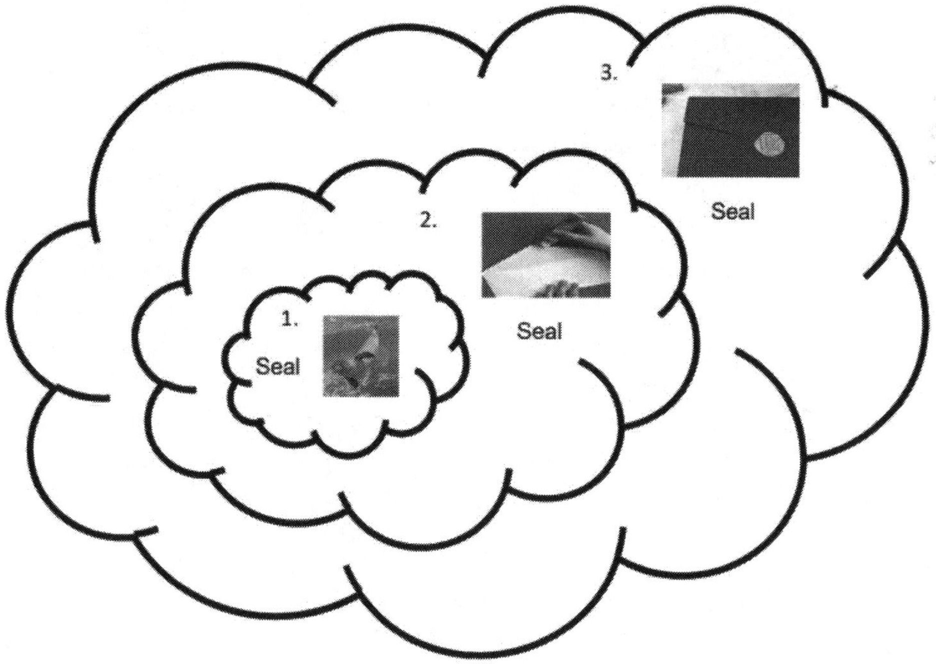

Figure 4f.2 Clouds of Understanding With Text

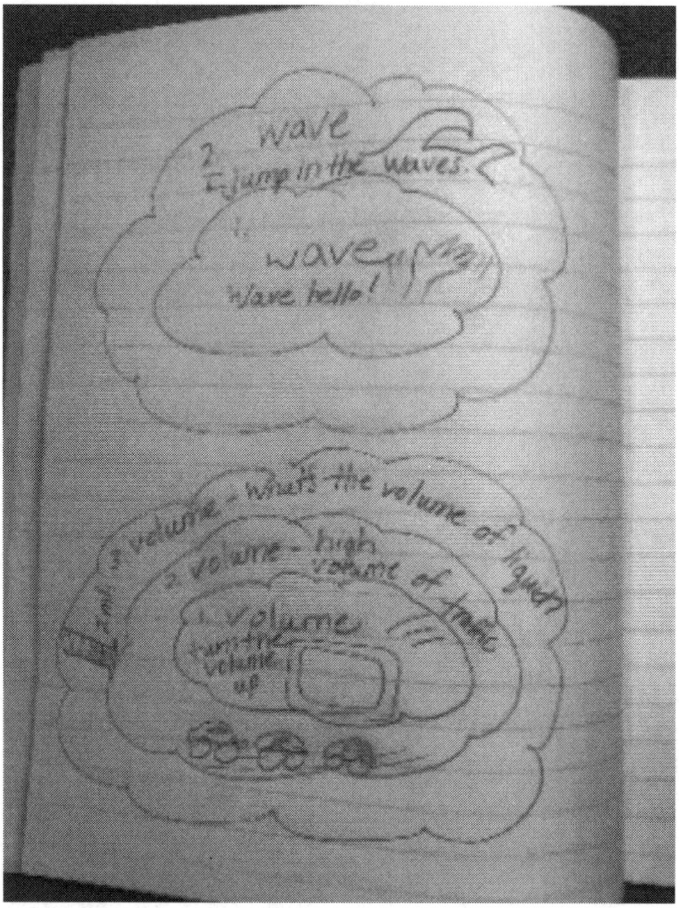

Figure 4f.3 Student Clouds of Meaning Notebook

meaning. Using concentric clouds, students can see that knowledge of multiple-meaning words is useful and increases our understanding of our world! In the example that follows, one cloud was drawn, starting with the most basic definition for the word "seal." Carmen added a second concentric cloud as students encountered the word "seal" as in to seal an envelope. Finally, in their study of the Revolutionary War, students learned that the King of England placed his "seal" of approval on the Stamp Act, prompting Carmen to draw a third concentric cloud to add yet another meaning of the word "seal" in a different context. This is an example of the three meanings of the word "seal." It was placed on chart paper and hung in the room as an anchor poster for future reference to multimeaning words.

Over time, as Carmen incorporated the clouds of meaning on a routine basis, her students knew immediately her intention when she would begin to draw a cloud on the board. The routine was securely in place, and the cloud served as a time-saving trigger, or signal, to her students that they were about to take a look at a multimeaning word.

Adaptations: For early learners, nonreaders/writers, and beginning English learners, pictures can be substituted for the written definitions to aid their comprehension. As you introduce the first word in a series of definitions for a multimeaning word, the cloud will again signal the relationship of the words. A simple sketch can be used to illustrate the words instead of a printed photo or picture.

Older students can use a notebook to record the multiple meaning words introduced by the teacher to the entire class as well as those encountered independently in reading.

Below is a sampling of common multiple meaning words by grade levels.

K–2

bark	bat	bowl	can	check	fair
last	lie	mean	park	play	ring
root	row	sink	star	swing	tire

Multiple Meaning Word	**Most Common Definition**	**Less Common Definitions**
bark		
play		
swing		

3–5

bear	bill	blue	change	ear	fork
handle	kind	log	note	pool	range
scale	shed	spring	store	train	yard

Multiple Meaning Word	**Most Common Definition**	**Less Common Definitions**
blue		
fork		
yard		

1. In the space, create a "clouds of meaning" anchor poster for your students using a multiple-meaning word that is specific to your grade level.

Tips for Working With ELs

As ESL teachers, Carmen and Kristen know English learners strongly need support in understanding multiple meaning words. Their students often understand the most common meanings of those words, so whenever they encounter a multiple meaning word, they defer to the most literal or common meaning. This can cause confusion, especially as the EL's vocabulary repertoire increases. Here is an example of a Developing EL questioning the teacher during a lesson.

Example Dialog 1:

Teacher: The birds delivered mail during the Revolutionary War.
Student A: Wait, what is **mail?**
Student B: You know, letters that come to your house.
Student A: Wait, I am **male**. I don't get it.
Teacher: (writes "mail" and "male" on the board): (Points to all the boys in the classroom and points to the word "male." Draws a quick sketch of a letter and points to "mail.")

The preceding is an example of how background knowledge can impede the learner so it is important for the teacher to address these misconceptions in the moment. As seen in the example above, homophones can be particularly confusing to ELs when they encounter them while they are reading. Therefore, it is important for teachers to seize on teachable moments when students encounter multiple meaning words during a lesson. When we teach in the moment, we address multiple meaning words in context rather than in isolation.

Let's take a look at another example. This time, the students encountered an example of a homonym in a social studies text.

Example Dialog 2:

Teacher: "A British soldier fired into the crowd." What does that sentence mean?
Student A: The soldier throw a bomb.
Student B: There was a fire.
Teacher: (to student A) Why do you think there was a bomb?
Student A: Bombs have fire. Fire is in the picture.
Teacher: (to student B) Why do you think there was a fire?
Student B: I see fire in the picture.
Teacher: Let's look at the photograph. What else do you see?
Student A: Soldiers and guns.
Teacher: Yes, and what do guns do?
Student B: Shoot!
Student A: So the soldiers shoot. Fire means shoot.

Reflection Activity

1. How does the students' background knowledge, in the two dialogues, impede their understanding of the words "male" and "mail" and "fire"?

   ____
   ____
   ____

2. What did the teacher do, in the examples, to help the students understand the difference between "male" and "mail" and the correct meaning of the word "fire?"

   ____
   ____
   ____

On-the-spot strategies when students encounter multiple meaning words:

1. Ask and answer questions like the teacher did in the examples.
2. Provide context clues for students.
3. Draw quick sketches to illustrate the definitions of multiple meaning words.

- Create an on-the-spot cloze activity such as the one below:
  - ◆ Houses caught on _____________ during the 1700s because there were no fire trucks or fire stations.
  - ◆ The soldiers _____________ their guns during battle.
  - ◆ A boss can _____________ a person for not doing their job.

References

Common Core State Standards Appendix A

Parent, K. (2012). The most frequent English homonyms. *RELC Journal: A Journal of Language Teaching and Research*, *43*(1), 69–81.

Strategy #7: Exposing Students to a Full Range of Signal Words at the Sentence Level

Strategy Focus

Signal words, or transition words, as they are commonly referred to, are essential to the effective organization of discourse. Oftentimes, students gain most of their practice with these words when writing, especially at the paragraph or essay level. In this chapter, teachers will become familiar with strategies to incorporate signal words that provide abundant oral practice with this vocabulary.

Strategy #7: Exposing Students to a Full Range of Signal Words at the Sentence Level

Introduction

Whether we are speaking or writing, transition words, or "signal words," as we will call them, help convey our thoughts in a clear way. They alert the listener or the reader to what's about to be presented, help with understanding the organization of our thoughts, and give prompts as to the relationship among ideas.

Description

The strategy of exposing students to a full range of signal words recognizes that there exists a body, or lexicon, of words and phrases all with the same function. Once students have been introduced to the most basic of signal words, teachers can capitalize on the fact that there are other more sophisticated words with similar functions that can be substituted in place of the more common ones. For example, when comparing two people, we might say, "Ramón has black hair, <u>but</u> Janessa has blond hair." The conjunction "but" serves as a signal to the reader or listener that a comparison is being made. The reflective teacher can, over time, replace "but" with other more elevated word forms with the same function. So, the example above becomes: "Ramón has black hair; <u>however,</u> Janessa has blond hair." This strategy requires teachers to deliberately replace common signal words with great frequency until each lexicon has been exhausted.

Rationale

What do students need to know? In order for students to be college and career ready, they will need the knowledge and skills connected to the standards. This knowledge includes, in part, the ability to compare and contrast ideas, express cause-and-effect relationships, and convey thoughts in discourse, both in speaking and in writing. Signal words play a key role in the major functions of language whether we are describing, explaining, presenting an argument, or comparing and contrasting. As such, students need to have a robust working knowledge of these academic words and not only those used in everyday social language.

What's the challenge? Many of us use the most basic of signal words, such as "and," "but," and "so." These words are commonly used in our social conversations, in emails, and in texts. Without a conscientious effort, teachers will continue to use these familiar words and phrases hundreds of times throughout the course of a week. Unfortunately, practices like these plateau our students' language growth. If we repeatedly provide our students with the same language input, we can most likely expect the same language output.

What does the strategy offer? This strategy offers scores of opportunities to model the use of elevated signal words to add additional information, to compare and contrast, and to show cause-and-effect relationships. As we provide this type of elevated language input, we will be equipping students with an understanding of the academic language found in textbooks as well as the ability to eventually use this register of language in their speaking and writing.

Ideas in Action

When first introducing the concept of signal words, they may be likened to a traffic signal. Carmen created the traffic light below to provide a visual representation of the concept. She displays the poster in a prominent place on a bulletin board. The traffic light visual serves two purposes. First, it serves as a reminder to the teacher to use signal words consistently as opportunities arise. Secondly, the visual reminds students, just like a traffic light, of what is to come for the listener or the reader. As mentioned earlier, signal words are crucial to our learners' vocabulary development as they are integrally connected to the standards and help with one's expression of thoughts in a sophisticated way.

After the visual is introduced, one of the best places to start, especially with young learners, is signal words for adding information. Typically,

Figure 4g.1 Dr. Rowe Teaching Signal Words With Her Signal Light Anchor Poster

in our everyday speech, we use the word "also" when giving more information on a topic. While "also" may suffice in a social conversation, it can quickly become redundant if we are giving a lot of information to someone or developing oral or written discourse. Additionally, if students are not exposed to more elevated forms of signal words, they will be less likely to understand them when encountering them in written text. They will also be less likely to use them in their writing. For this reason, we will want to use a variety of signal words to keep our listeners' or readers' attention.

When introducing the alternate signal words, it can be advantageous to introduce the entire lexicon at one time. This serves two purposes: (1) it makes students aware that the words go together because they serve a common function, in this case, to alert others that more information is about to be shared; and (2) it provides all students an equitable opportunity to accelerate language at their own rate of comfortability. Many factors go into how quickly students will acquire new vocabulary and move through the stages of recognizing the word to understanding its use in context to using it themselves in their speaking and writing. Presenting all of the words guarantees that we keep the ceiling of opportunity high for those students wanting to experiment with the new vocabulary.

Signal Words for Adding More Information
Also
In addition
Furthermore
Equally important
Additionally
. . . as well
Moreover
Not only . . . but also

When introducing students to this lexicon of signal words in your own speech, consider using a topic or scenario that is familiar to your students. For example, recounting the details of your weekend is a good way to model the new academic vocabulary. When modeling, be sure to use a variety of signal words in your speaking and to call students' attention to them by speaking them slowly and deliberately. A sample oral paragraph follows;

On Saturday, we drove to the grocery store to buy food for my daughter's baby shower. We bought hamburgers, hot dogs, and potato chips. In addition, we bought some pink balloons because we knew she was going to have a girl. Equally important, we picked up a special cake at the bakery that said, "Congratulations on your new little bundle soon to arrive." The party was loads of fun. Everyone not only had plenty to eat, but also enjoyed themselves thoroughly!

Put It Into Practice

Now it's your turn! Choose one of the prompts that follow and write out a paragraph of four to five sentences that you can recite orally to your students to introduce signal words for adding information.

Prompts:

- What did you do over the weekend?
- What are the most important qualities of a successful student?
- What will you do this summer?

____
____
____
____
____
____
____
____

How can we connect this strategy to writing?

Rotating Review Using Signal Words

Materials needed:

- Index cards with signal words on them
- A short informational text

Directions:

1. Students read text independently and highlight the key details.
2. Create groups of three to four students.
3. Distribute one signal word card (each card will have a different signal word) to each student.
4. Students take turns providing a summary of the text using key details. Each student adds one key detail using the signal word for adding information on their card.
5. After everyone has had a turn to add information using their card, shuffle the cards.
6. Repeat the activity.

The oral activity gives students practice with the new vocabulary. Students have multiple exposures of hearing the vocabulary in context as well as trying it on in their oral language.

How do you go about teaching the different syntax structures for the various signal words for adding information?

Figure 4g.2 Signal Word Rotating Oral Review

Most of the signal words for adding information require that the signal word be placed at the beginning of the sentence that provides more information. In the case of ". . . as well," the signal comes at the end of the added information. The ". . . not only . . . but also . . ." structure is the most difficult because it requires a parallel structure. In other words, both pieces of information must be the same part of speech.

In sentence A, the girl is described using a verb, and more information is added using another verb. In sentence B, the girl is described using an adjective, and more information is added using another adjective. In this way, the structure of the sentence remains parallel.

A. The girl not only <u>sings</u> but also <u>dances</u>.
B. The girl is not only <u>athletic</u> but also <u>intelligent</u>.

In order to aid in the teaching of these signal words with more difficult syntactical structures, Carmen uses the activity that follows.

Human Sentences Activity

Materials:

1. Large flash cards
2. Black and red Sharpie markers

Directions:

1. Write "not only" and "but also" with the red Sharpie on two separate index cards.
2. Distribute one card to each student volunteer.
3. With the help of the class, decide the correct order in which students should stand to form a grammatically correct sentence.

Following are examples of how you could create the flash cards.

***The activity can be done by the whole group or in small groups. If small groups are used, then each group will need their own set of cards. If you are introducing the not only . . . but also structure for the first time, it is

The	girl	not only	sings	but also	dances

Figure 4g.3 Not Only/But Also Example 1

The	girl	is	not only	athletic	but also	intelligent

Figure 4g.4 Not Only/But Also Example 2

best to engage in the human sentences activity with the whole group so that any errors in syntax can be corrected.

For concepts difficult for students to master, the authors believe students benefit from seeing signal words in written form. In addition, interacting with peers in small groups provides an opportunity for students to negotiate meaning using the new vocabulary. In other words, the students have the opportunity to experiment with the language in order to gain practice with a complex syntax, or word order.

Promoting Signal Words in Students' Reading and Writing

Marco Ortiz, elementary ESL teacher and co-teacher of intermediate grades, reminds students of the many options for the common signal words for "and," "but," and "so." During the writing process, Marco routinely reinforces the need to use a variety of words in place of the more common ones. To aid students in the process, he created the document that follows.

This document could be accessed as a desk document or an anchor chart that hangs in the classroom for all students to refer to when speaking or writing.

	and
We ate pasta for dinner,	**and** we had cake for dessert.
We ate pasta for dinner.	**Additionally**, we had cake for dessert.
We ate pasta for dinner.	**Also**, we had cake for dessert.
We ate pasta for dinner.	**Furthermore**, we had cake for dessert.
We ate pasta for dinner.	**Moreover**, we had cake for dessert.
We ate pasta for dinner.	**In addition**, we had cake for dessert.
We ate pasta for dinner.	We had cake for dessert, **too**.
We ate pasta for dinner.	We had cake for dessert, **as well**.
	but
I can't walk fast,	**but** I can walk for a long time.
I can't walk fast.	**However**, I can walk for a long time.
I can't walk fast.	**Yet**, I can walk for a long time.
I can't walk fast.	**Even so**, I can walk for a long time.
I can't walk fast.	**Still**, I can walk for a long time.
I can't walk fast.	**Nevertheless**, I can walk for a long time.
I can't walk fast.	**Nonetheless**, I can walk for a long time.
	so
It was raining outside,	**so** we stayed inside for recess.
It was raining outside.	**As a result**, we stayed inside for recess.
It was raining outside.	**Therefore**, we stayed inside for recess.
It was raining outside.	**Hence**, we stayed inside for recess.
It was raining outside.	**Thus**, we stayed inside for recess.
It was raining outside.	**Ergo**, we stayed inside for recess.

Figure 4g.5 Writing Resource for Signal Words

Another alternative is to create mini flash cards and put them all on a ring for students to access when they are writing. Organizing them by their function is easiest for students. The categories of signal words can be further organized by color-coding the cards whereby each color represents a different function. Students can use the ring as a resource as they write.

Because the syntax, or word order, used with some of the signal words is more complex than others, it is best to start with the more simple structures first with younger learners. Carmen told her second-grade students that they were no longer going to use the second-grade word "also." Instead, they would be using college words like "further" and "additionally" whenever they wanted to give more information about a topic. Her students felt not only smart but also empowered to be able to express themselves using robust vocabulary!

Figure 4g.6 Signal Words on a Ring

Following are two charts that can be used with younger and older elementary students.

Signal Words for . . .
Adding Information (Also)

Furthermore
Equally Important
Moreover
Further
In addition
Additionally

Figure 4g.7 Replacing Also With Elevated Language for Primary Grades

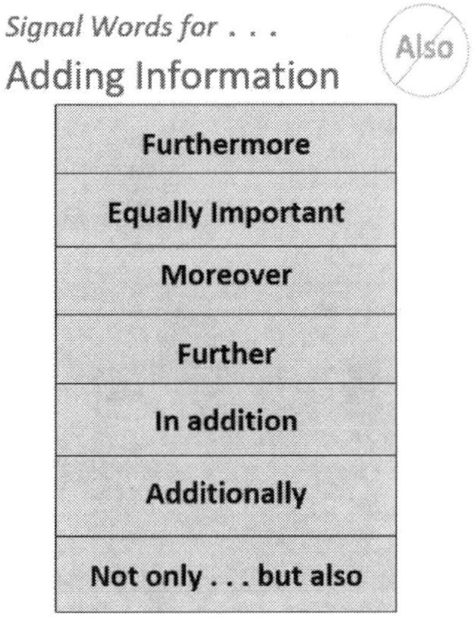

Figure 4g.8 Replacing Also With Elevated Language for Intermediate Grades

Tips for Working With ELs

English learners will need many repetitions of the new vocabulary and sentence structures before producing them in their productive language. In addition to teachers modeling signal words in oral discourse, they can reinforce students' acquisition of the new language by providing the tabletop placemats or flash cards of the new words and phrases as a guide during writing. The authors have found that students feel empowered to use "big" words in their speaking and writing.

In addition to seeing writing reminders of the signal words, English learners will also benefit from appropriate voice inflection, also referred to as the use of prosody. When modeling these signal words in speech, teachers should overemphasize these words initially. In addition, reading them a bit more slowly than the other words in the sentence will also help draw the students' attention to the words. For example:

- "It's raining; ***therefore***, we will be having recess indoors."
- "You will need to explain how you got the correct answer. ***In addition***, you will need to use math vocabulary."
- "Today is pajama day, ***whereas*** tomorrow is favorite book character day."

Now, read each sentence aloud, practicing placing emphasis and slowed speech for each underlined word.

Using Gestures to Aid Comprehension

In the video clip that follows, Carmen demonstrates how comprehensible input can be provided to English learners through the use of gesturing when using signal words. She models this strategy with two basic conjunctions, "but" and "so." Using these types of gestures coupled with substitutionary language is a powerful way to help bolster the language of all students but especially English learners.

Using Hand Motions to Support the Modeling of Signal Words

Reflection Questions

1. How will you ensure that your students have access to the signal words that you have modeled in your speech as they engage in writing activities? ____________________

2. How will you hold them accountable for using the signal words in their speaking and writing?
____

Strategy #8: Bolstering Our Speech With Literary Devices

Strategy Focus

Similes, metaphors, personification, and idioms are among a few of the types of figurative language pervasive in the English language. Oftentimes, students are first introduced to this rich language in written texts. In this chapter, the reader will become familiar with ways of introducing and reinforcing figurative language in an effort to enhance their descriptions, oral and written.

Strategy #8: Bolstering Our Speech With Literary Devices

Infusing academic language into my everyday language is key to me. I use it with my students from when they arrive in the morning to when they leave in the afternoon.

Using academic language outside of direct instruction normalizes using that kind of speech or vocabulary throughout all aspects or areas of one's life.

~Ben Jackson, Fourth Grade Teacher
(B. Jackson, personal communication, May 15, 2022)

Introduction

Many great orators such as Martin Luther King, Winston Churchill, and John F. Kennedy used literary devices in their speeches. Dr. King used alliteration when he spoke these famous words, "not judged by the color of their skin but by the content of their character." Winston Churchill also used alliteration when he stated, "your grisly gang who work your wicked will" in his speech "We Shall Fight on the Beaches." Declaring Americans would take charge of the space program, John F. Kennedy used this metaphor: "America has tossed its cap over the wall of space." The use of literary devices in our everyday speech has the potential to have a lasting impact. The listeners often remember speeches peppered with metaphors, similes, alliteration, and other literary devices.

Description

This strategy incorporates the use of selected literary devices and literary terms in teachers' speech. Teachers will be given a list of literary devices, their definitions, and examples. They will have the opportunity to select literary devices that are specific to their grade level and infuse examples of these literary techniques into their everyday speech.

Rationale

What do students need to know? By the end of their elementary career, students need to be able to recognize many literary devices in both reading and writing. For example, in English language arts, the reader must be able to interpret figurative language in order to comprehend characters and their actions. Students will also need to be familiar with literary terms such as "antagonist" and "protagonist."

What's the challenge? While we may hear figurative language and examples of literary devices during social interactions, we may not hear a full range of each type. Many students have not had repeated exposures orally to figurative language or literary terms; therefore, the concepts are more difficult to grasp when first introduced through literature.

What does the strategy offer? This strategy offers an opportunity for teachers to introduce literary devices such as figurative language before they are expected to explicitly teach it. Teachers will be given tips on how and when to bolster their speech by modeling literary devices throughout the school day.

Ideas in Action

The best way to learn the meanings of figurative language is to be exposed to it on a regular basis. Carmen cites her husband, Rick, as a master of using figurative language: "As our children were growing up, he used figurative language extensively, modeling it for our children. While they did not know the names for the various types, they clearly understood that language could be used in creative ways to make strong and powerful impacts for the listener."

Carmen shares three examples of her children's original use of figurative language to make a strong point.

"A few specks in a piece of gold"

Our son, Joshua, was in elementary school when one of his teachers assigned a multi-paragraph writing assignment to her students. Our son, Joshua, completed the assignment and handed it in, only to have the teacher tell him that he would need to rewrite his essay with the spelling errors corrected. Our son responded to his teacher's request with the following metaphor, "If you had a piece of gold with a few specks in it, would you throw it out?"

Carmen notes that whether or not she agrees with her son challenging his teacher's request, she admits he creatively proposed an alternative view. Through the use of a metaphor, he was able to portray his own feelings regarding the situation in a softer tone than had he come right out and expressed to the teacher his disdain toward the request.

"Worse than a 1,000 bee stings"

When Carmen's three youngest sons, Peter, Danny, and Gabe, were young, it gave her great joy to dress them alike. One Sunday morning, the oldest of the three, Peter, who was five years old at the time, looked her in the eye and said, "Mom, when you dress us all alike, it's worse than 1,000 bee stings."

He could have simply stated that he didn't like it when she dressed him and his brothers alike, but when he used an exaggerated metaphor of comparing it to the unfortunate event of a bee sting, let alone 1,000 of them, she got the message loud and clear!

"Which child do you love most?"

When our son, Gabe, was a busy middle school student, Carmen asked him which activity he enjoyed the most, soccer or music. His response was short and to the point, using the following simile: "That's like asking me which child I love best."

Before we get started diving into the strategies, let's take a look at 10 different types of figurative language and a few literary devices often used in literature.

What are the 10 types of figurative language?

Figurative Language Types		
Type	**Definition**	**Example**
Simile	A form of speech that compares two concepts by using the connecting words "like" or "as"	• Busy as a bee • Cool as a cucumber
Metaphor	A form of speech that compares two concepts without the use of the connecting words "like" or "as"	• Shining star • He's a brick wall. (referring to a goalie who doesn't let balls get past)
Personification	The attribution of a personal nature or human characteristic to something nonhuman	• The curtains danced in the wind.

(continued)

Figurative Language Types		
Type	**Definition**	**Example**
Hyperbole	Exaggerated statement not to be taken literally	• I'm so hungry I could eat a horse.
Allusion	An expression to call something to mind without mentioning it specifically	• It's your big day. (referring to someone's wedding day) • Pandora's box
Idioms	A group of words established by usage as having a meaning not being defined by the individual words	• It's raining cats and dogs. • I'm feeling blue today.
Pun	A joke exploiting the different possible meanings of a word	• Donut give up. • Words cannot expresso how I feel about you.
Onomatopoeia	The formation of a word from a sound associated by what is named	• Sizzle • Crackle • Rumble
Alliteration	The occurrence of the same letter or sound at the beginning of adjacent or closely related words	• Peter Piper picked a peck of pickled peppers.
Oxymoron	A figure of speech in which contradictory terms appear together	• Bittersweet • Adult children • Jumbo shrimp • Current history

Reflection Question

1. Did you know all of these terms? If not, which ones were unfamiliar to you?

____

____

____

Literary Toolbox

In addition to modeling literary techniques in our speech, we also want to encourage students to try the techniques on for size. To this end, Carmen

Figure 4h.1 Literary Device Toolboxes

purchased a small plastic toolbox complete with an array of plastic tools. The toolbox is labeled "Literary Tools" on one side and "Literary Techniques" on the other side. In this way, students learn the various forms of the term. Then, each tool is labeled with one of the 10 literary devices to remind students that as narrative writers, they have an array of tools at their disposal.

Literary Terms

Remember, not all literary terms need to be confined to the English language arts (ELA) classroom. During an ELA unit, fourth-grade teacher Ben Jackson realized his students were going to need to have a deep knowledge of the literary terms "antagonist" and "protagonist." In order to develop that deep understanding, Ben decided he was going to make a conscious effort to use those terms outside the ELA classroom. He capitalized on the importance of bolstering his teacher talk through strategic modeling. Here, Ben explains in his own words how he does this:

> *One example [of using literary terms outside of the ELA instruction block] that has stood out from this year is describing students as protagonists and antagonists. While teaching character types in reading instruction, I made sure to define a protagonist as someone who is solving conflict and the antagonist as someone who is causing conflict (not simply the good guy or the bad guy). Since my students seemed to have a good grasp on those vocabulary words, I started celebrating students that were problem solving and working to figure things out as protagonists and playfully warning students that were starting drama or fights, "Don't be the antagonist!" I also connected the verb "to antagonize" to students, and I inwardly smile each time I hear a student say, "Mister, she's antagonizing me!" as I go to put out another fire of social conflict.*

Ben is a fourth-grade teacher. Think of important literary devices your students need to master. They may differ across grade levels and content areas.

Put It Into Practice

1. Make a list of these terms, their definitions, and examples using the chart provided.

Terms	Definitions	Examples

2. How can you infuse examples of these terms or concepts into your everyday interactions with your students?

 ____

 ____

Ben provides another example of how he bolsters vocabulary through teacher talk. Read the excerpt to see how he does this during a read-aloud.

> *When I read aloud to my students outside of ELA lessons (as a cool-down activity after recess, for example), it is important to me that I don't alter or dumb down any vocabulary. I am currently reading* James and the Giant Peach *with my fourth graders, and in addition to rigorous and academic language, Roald Dahl uses a lot of antiquated terms and British vernacular. This forces even my high achievers with large vocabularies to practice their context clue skills. After reading a paragraph with challenging vocabulary, I will stop and check in with everyone, making sure to allow students a chance to reason out meaning before just giving them the answers.*

While the focus of this book is on authentic teacher talk and not teaching vocabulary explicitly, teachers can use the vocabulary presented in read-alouds as a springboard for modeling the elevated language in their everyday speech. The authors encourage teachers to pull out the rich vocabulary encountered during read-alouds and make a point to use it soon after.

Using Metaphor and Simile

Similes and metaphors are a great way to highlight similarities between two items in an interesting and creative way. While similes are more explicit using "like" or "as," metaphors are more implicit in making comparisons.

The use of these figures of speech can spark interest and create a strong image for the listener. Following are similes and metaphors that could easily be used in a school setting.

Similes
He's as good as gold.
She's as cool as a cucumber.
They fought like cats and dogs.
He's as strong as an ox.
She's as quiet as a mouse.
He's as busy as a bee.
She's as sharp as a tack.
You are growing like a weed.
He's as silent as the grave.
She runs like the wind!

Metaphors
That's music to my ears.
He's a walking encyclopedia.
The world is your oyster.
That computer is a dinosaur.
This class is a three-ring circus sometimes.
You girls are two peas in a pod.
Words can cut deeper than a knife.
You're a shining star.
He's a rock.
Life is a rollercoaster.

Put It Into Practice

1. Pulling out vocabulary during a read-aloud is not the only way to bolster students' vocabulary. Consider a read-aloud that you use with your students. While reading, stop to highlight and clarify any literary devices. When the read-aloud is over, look for opportunities,

during the same day if possible, to use those same literary devices again. Students will benefit from hearing them used again in a new context!

In the chart that follows, what were some of the literary devices you encountered in your read-aloud? Complete the chart below.

Type of Literary Device	**Example From the Text or Media**	**How Did You Reinforce the Example in a New Context?**
Example: idiom	She stole an upward glance. (referring to a character who quickly looked at another character)	"I see you stealing a glance at our snack." (referring to a student who is looking at our snack)

Using Literary Devices When Giving Directions

Third-grade teacher Lenore Charnock uses figurative language when she is describing what the classroom should look like and sound like during readers' workshop. In the example that follows, she compares reading workshop to being on an airplane. Here is how she frames her instructions as her students transition:

> *How many of you have been on an airplane before? How many of you have traveled on an airplane without an adult or other family member? So, I want you to imagine that you are all traveling by air today. What should your position be? Where should you be? "Sitting in a seat." Should you be reclining on the floor? "No." Should your legs be out in the aisle? "No." So before the plane takes off, the pilot says, "Have your seat in the upright position. Your tray table should be up." Both feet on the floor while you read today. Make sure your back is as straight as a ruler. Sitting up nice and tall. Don't be leaning into your seatmate's space. If you are reading on your electronic device, that is fine, but hold it in front of you. You should be confined in your own space and as quiet as a mouse. Noticing that one student was leaning on a classmate's desk, she noted, "OK, that is not correct. You are invading your seatmate's space." That is not permitted on an airplane.*

Reflection Question

1. Summarize how Lenore used metaphor in order to give directions.

____

____

____

Putting It Into Practice

2. You're getting ready to walk your students to the cafeteria for lunch. Provide students with literary devices to help them imagine they are having a five-star-restaurant dining experience. The chart that follows breaks down the experience into individual components. Feel free to add components to suit your students' needs!

Creating a Five-Star-Restaurant Experience in the Cafeteria	
Getting in line	As we get in line, we will not be jockeying for positions like racehorses. We need to be responsible jockeys (people who racehorses) and take our position in line.
Walking into the cafeteria	Don't walk into the restaurant like a bull in a china closet. Rather, walk in as quietly as a mouse.
Greeting the staff	
Ordering your food	
Sitting at your table	
Talking with your friends	
Making requests	

Catching the Students' Attention Using Alliteration

Alliteration should not be overlooked! This particular type of figurative language grabs the listener's attention, not to mention that it's fun. Kristen uses it in third grade when students practice using money in order to bolster vocabulary across the curriculum. Kristen calls her store "Happy Haase's Holiday

Hide-Away" and makes a point to repeat the store's name to each group of students who rotate through her store. Students' first reaction is to be humored. Some ask why she gave her store that name. Kristen asks them what they notice about the name. This opens the door for a quick, in-the-moment conversation. Kristen loves modeling alliteration, and this is a perfect opportunity, without missing a beat, to expose students to another type of figurative language.

Alliteration and Adjectives

Using students' names to introduce the concept of alliteration is a good place to start. Some examples are "Fantastic and fabulous fraction Feona" and "Melodious, money-making Mohammed." These are examples of using alliteration across the curriculum; however, teachers can also use alliteration in the English arts classroom to cement character traits as well as promote positive attributes of the students.

Put It Into Practice

1. Using the list of positive character traits that follows, complete the class roster so you can practice using alliteration with your students. At the beginning of the year, you may start with just the student's name and one attribute. As the year progresses and you get to know your students better, add to the list of attributes you attach to their names. While our list highlights character attributes, consider adding physical attributes, hobbies, talents, and any other features that shine a spotlight on their uniqueness.

Positive Character Attributes

active adventurous affectionate ambitious appreciative attentive
brave brilliant careful caring charismatic charming clever
compassionate competitive concerned confident conscientious
considerate consistent cooperative courageous curious
dependable determined eager easygoing efficient empathetic
energetic enthusiastic fair faithful friendly funny generous
gentle gregarious happy-go-lucky hopeful humble humorous
imaginative independent innovative intelligent insistent jovial
likable logical lovable loyal mature melodious obedient
observant optimistic open-minded peaceful persistent pleasant
polite prompt proud punctual quick quiet reliable respectful
resilient resourceful responsible self-reliant silly sincere skillful
smart sociable studious scholarly sweet talented talkative
thoughtful tolerant trusting trustworthy virtuous warm
warm-hearted willful wise witty

Student Names	Alliteration Attributes

Final Put-It-Into-Practice Activity!

2. In this strategy, you have been exposed to a myriad of literary techniques. Can you provide an additional example of each type of figurative language? Add your examples to the chart. Now, make a resolution to model this language in your teacher talk.

Figurative Language Types	
Type	Example
Simile	
Metaphor	
Personification	
Hyperbole	
Allusion	
Idiom	
Pun	
Onomatopoeia	
Alliteration	
Oxymoron	

Tips for Working With ELs

Using figurative language with a student who is beginning to learn English should be done cautiously. It is important for teachers of these students to use figurative language in a context. However, students with a solid grasp of social language need to be exposed to figurative language on a regular basis. Unfortunately, ELs' first exposure to this type of language is usually in reading and writing. What if teachers could begin to build an understanding orally before students are exposed to it in more academic settings?

Strategy #9: Capitalizing on Root Words and Their Family Members

Strategy Focus

Understanding word families, groups of words that have a common root, is a great skill to have in order to decipher new words. Roots, prefixes, and suffixes are many times introduced to students through written text. This delays equipping students with this skill until they are able to read. In this chapter, educators will be given strategies to use to introduce students to word families through oral language, in context.

Strategy #9 Capitalizing on Root Words and Their Family Members

Introduction

All students need to continually grow their vocabularies in order to be ultimately college and career ready. Goodwin et al. (2013) found that there exists a reciprocal relationship between a student's knowledge of morphology, such as roots, prefixes, and suffixes, and reading comprehension.

Description

Words with the same root, or base word, are sometimes said to belong to the same "word family." To avoid confusion with the 37 word families such as "ack," "ike," "ight," used when teaching students how to read, the authors from this point on will refer to word families as root words and their related family members. Recognizing that root words may utilize different prefixes or suffixes, we introduce these words as well so that students become familiar with entire word families. To implement the strategy, teachers need to identify words within the same family, those that share a common root. Once they have been identified, teachers bolster their speech through strategic modeling that includes various members of the word family in order to help students see a relationship among the words.

Rationale

What do students need to know? The National Reading Panel (NICHHD, 2000) found that vocabulary is essential for students to learn to read and comprehend the text.

What's the challenge? The amount of academic words to be taught abounds, and as a result, teachers find the task daunting. But what if there were a way to streamline the process of teaching academic vocabulary?

What does the strategy offer? Helping students gain an awareness of roots and affixes within word families is one way to help build their vocabulary. By modeling common Greek and Latin roots, teachers can bolster students' language exponentially. In addition, after gaining knowledge of morphology, the smallest parts of words that carry meaning, students can then begin to transfer this skill to attack the meaning of unfamiliar words.

Ideas in Action

To get started, identify a group of words within the same word family so that you can capitalize on the relationship among these words with a common root. If you need help getting started, the QR code that follows will give you access to an excellent resource that lists hundreds of academic word families: the Academic Word Lists (Coxhead, 2000). These Tier 2 words, which are used across content areas, are guaranteed to give students the repeated exposure in different contexts needed to acquire new vocabulary words.

Coxhead's Academic Word Lists

Prefixes and suffixes are the smallest word parts that contain meaning.

- Prefixes, word parts attached to the beginning of words, have the ability to change a word's meaning.
- Suffixes, word parts attached to the end of words, can change the meaning of a word or even its part of speech.

Here is a list of the most common affixes. The four most frequent prefixes account for 97% of the prefixed and suffixed words in printed school English.

Prefixes			**Suffixes**		
Prefix	**Meaning**	**example**	**suffix**	**meaning**	**Example**
dis-	not, opposite of	disagree	-ed	past-tense verbs	helped
in-/ im-/ir-	not	injustice, impossible irrelevant	-ing	participle	running
re-	again	realign	-ly	characteristic of	lovely
un-	not	unkind	-s/-es	plural form of nouns, more than one	books, boxes

In addition to the examples, the authors feel it is important to model vocabulary that contains a full range of prefixes and suffixes in order to expand students' vocabularies. Helping increase our students' knowledge of roots, prefixes, and suffixes can help expand their knowledge of words and give them a tool for deciphering new words.

Here are some examples:

Prefix/Root Word/Suffix	Meaning	Part of Speech
predict (root word)	meaning to say what might happen in the future	Verb
prediction (root word + suffix)	what was said that might happen	Noun
predictor (root word + suffix)	a person or thing that says what might happen in the future	Noun
predictable (root word + suffix)	able to be predicted	Adjective
unpredictable (prefix + root word + suffix)	not able to be predicted	Adjective

Now let's consider, for example, the word "congregate" from an earlier chapter. Once a word has been chosen, the next step is to brainstorm a list of all of the other words within that word family that have the same root or word part.

con = together, with; greg = flock, group
Congregate
Congregation
Congregating
Congregates
Congregated
Recongregate

The chart that follows shows an example of how these words from a related word family could be modeled. The chart shows how teachers can leverage students' knowledge of one word by modeling the words from the same root family. As you will see, teachers can build students' vocabulary through repetition in a short period of time. Parts of speech and verb tenses can be modeled strategically in context to aid students' comprehension of the vocabulary.

Introduction Word: congregate		
	Sentence	**Part of Speech/Function**
1	"Let's congregate on the carpet."	Verb (command)
2	"I see you are congregating."	Verb (present progressive)
3	"You congregated quietly."	Verb (past tense)
4	"I see one congregant has not made her way over to the carpet yet."	Noun (suffix -ant)
5	"We made a congregation!"	Noun (suffix -tion)
6	"We will recongregate later this afternoon."	Verb (future tense, prefix -re)

Modeling sentences with the same root family is a great way to bolster students' language and, at the same time, expose them to the concept of word families. In the example, it might take the teacher a matter of seconds to speak each of the six sentences. But with repeated exposure to these words and others with similar roots, word parts, and inflections, students will expand their vocabularies and come to understand that some words function as verbs and others as nouns.

Put It Into Practice

Now it's your turn!

1. Choose a word that is part of a word family that will be your introduction word and write the word at the top of the chart.
2. Create a sentence with your root word in the chart beside row #1.
3. Choose one to three additional words from the word family and write them in sentences in the chart on rows #2, #3, and #4.
4. Identify the part of speech, or function, of the words from your word family.
   Here are some examples you could use to help you get started, or select your own:
   – scholar, assemble, construct, visual

Introduction/Root Word:		
	Sentence	**Part of Speech/Function**
1		
2		
3		
4		

Once you have worked through this activity, seize an upcoming opportunity to model the words for your students. Think of how, in the moment, you could use each of the forms so that they would most appropriately aid your students' understanding of that particular word in the word family.

To summarize, as teachers raise their own awareness of roots, prefixes, and affixes, they can then begin to identify them and seize opportunities to use them in their own speech throughout the day. As a result, teachers' modeling of words exposes students to the richness of language and the concept of word relationships.

Introducing Roots, Prefixes, and Suffixes to Students

The Common Core State Standards require students in second grade to "decode words with common prefixes and suffixes" and students in first grade to "read words with inflectional endings." Through the use of strategic modeling, teachers can introduce roots and affixes at an early age without explicitly teaching what they mean.

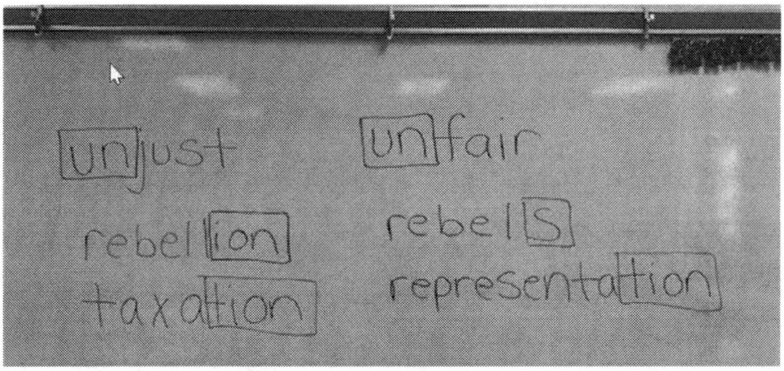

Figure 4i.1 Teaching Suffixes and Prefixes and Suffixes on the Spot

The authors also encourage teachers to use words with prefixes and suffixes across the content areas. For example, in social studies, students may encounter words such as "unfair" and "unjust." Here is an opportunity for organic, on-the-spot teaching. Kristen, when preparing for a social studies lesson, noticed many of the words that the students would encounter contained prefixes and suffixes. Instead of teaching an explicit lesson on prefixes, she decided she would address them in the moment. For example, when teaching the first lesson on the Boston Tea Party, she wrote the words "unfair" and "unjust"; "taxation without representation"; "rebels" and "rebellion." Notice how she picked key concepts from the unit.

In less than a minute, she wrote the words on the board and circled the prefixes and suffixes. Then she explained what the root words meant and the definitions of the prefixes and suffixes. That was it; then she moved on. Later, she will circle back to this teaching point when the opportunity presents itself to introduce additional words within the word families, having already laid a foundation.

Creating Interest Among Students for Roots and Their Related Words

One of the best ways to create interest and excitement for word families is as you use them in your own speech, begin to add emphasis to the roots and affixes, even drawing out the pronunciation so as to draw your students' attention to the word families' features. For younger children, add hand gestures and facial expressions when appropriate.

Seize opportunities throughout the school day to use roots, prefixes, and suffixes. For example, once students have been exposed to the prefix "re," you can ask them to help you determine the meaning of the word, "readjust." Perhaps you could adjust a scarf or the straps on a backpack or their

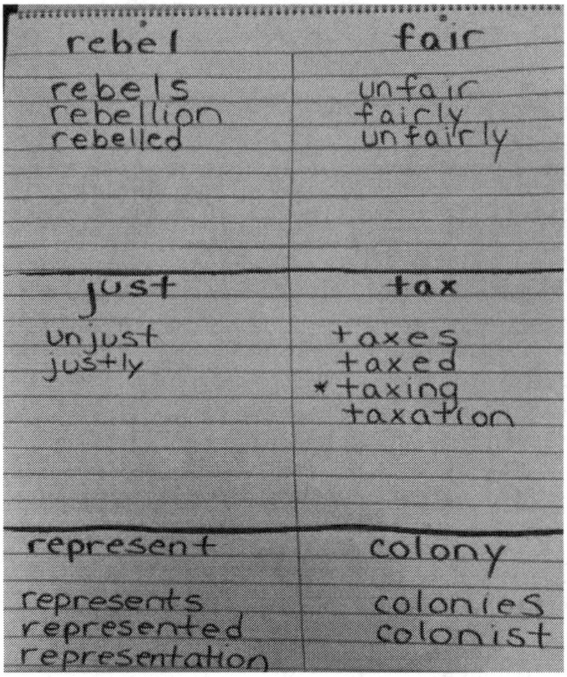

Figure 4i.2 Capitalizing on Root Families in the Social Studies Classroom

positions. Have all students engage in the same action. Then ask students what it means if I readjust the straps on my backpack. Then have all of your students repeat the action. In this way, students will very quickly learn the meaning of the affixes.

Connecting to Writing

Once you make the modeling of the use of word families a staple in your classroom, you will be able to help students transfer this new skill to pronounce new words with similar roots, prefixes, or suffixes, as well as spell unfamiliar words. When spelling new words, ask students what words or word parts they hear. Because of students' prior exposure as you have modeled these features of language, they will also be able to hear and isolate the individual word parts and roots.

Challenging students to use word family vocabulary in their writing is another way to help students move their word knowledge from the receptive to the productive realm. Carmen used "literacy notebooks" with her students in which they recorded their new learning about words, skills, and strategies. A section of the notebook was dedicated to roots and affixes. These notebooks

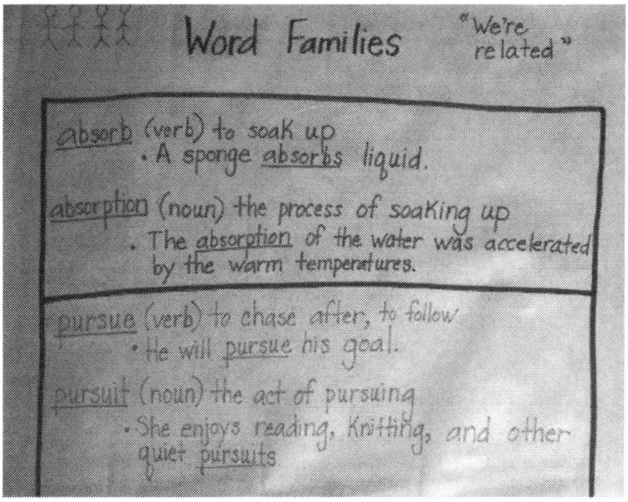

Figure 4i.3 Word Family Anchor Charts

became useful resources for students as they developed their listening, speaking, reading, and writing skills.

Tips for Working With ELs

English learners need to catch up with their native-English-speaking peers with respect to vocabulary. Modeling root words and their affixes can help develop ELs' vocabularies exponentially by focusing on the depth of words within families as opposed to only concentrating on developing the breadth of vocabularies, which is often the focus.

According to research, English learners with limited vocabularies benefitted from being equipped with morphology, or word-part, skills. Kieffer and Lesaux (2007) researched the impact of teaching morphology skills to English learners in an urban district and found that "students with greater understanding of morphology are more successful at learning academic vocabulary and comprehending text is a strong argument for including morphology instruction in language and literacy programs, especially in urban settings" (p. 139).

Extension Activities

For our elementary students in second grade and above, strategies in which students can see the word families in print are helpful. Teachers can create anchor posters together with students as they encounter words belonging to a word family, such as the one Carmen created:

During independent reading, students will encounter many new words. Frequently, teachers will use some type of graphic organizer to capture those words and to provide a place for students to record their inferences about the new word meanings. Teachers should consider providing a place on the new-word log for students to record any related words they can think of that are in the same word family. An example of such a word log:

New Word	What I Think it Means	The Word in a Sentence	Related Words in the Same Word Family
legislature	a group that makes laws	Our legislature passed a law requiring people to wear safety belts.	• legislator • legislation • legislative
persist	to keep going	If you persist, you will succeed.	• persistence • persisted • persisting

References

Coxhead, A. (2000). *Academic word list*. Victoria University of Wellington.

Goodwin, A. P., Huggins, A. C., Carlo, M. S., August, D., & Calderon, M. (2013). Minding morphology: How morphological awareness relates to reading for English language learners. *Reading and Writing, 26*(9), 1387–1415.

Kieffer, M. J., & Lesaux, N. K. (2007). Breaking down words to build meaning: Morphology, vocabulary, and reading comprehension in the urban classroom. *The Reading Teacher, 61*(2), 134–144.

National Institute of Child Health and Human Development. (2000). *Report of the national reading panel. Teaching children to read: An evidence-based assessment of the scientific research literature on reading and its implications for reading instruction (NIH Publication No. 00–4769).* U.S. Government Printing Office.

Strategy #10: Modeling Elevated Language at the Discourse Level

Strategy Focus

Students are listening to our speech not only at the word and sentence level but also at the discourse level. Through reflective teaching that considers the purpose of our language use, we can tailor our explanations, summaries, descriptions, arguments, and other discourse in ways that intentionally model academic discourse to our students. Think of the opportunities you have to connect with students about their interests: before or after class, during homeroom, on the playground, and in study hall. These moments offer opportunities to use specific vocabulary that relates to their interests. This chapter offers strategies on how to make the most of those impromptu conversations.

Strategy #10: Modeling Elevated Language at the Discourse Level

One of my favorite times of the day is the morning when the students first enter the building, especially on a Monday. I have the opportunity to ask them about their weekends. By asking about their weekends, I get to know them better as individuals and gain insight into what they enjoy doing with their families and outside the school building. Since we are talking about them, the conversation allows the students to share their background knowledge and with my response, they are able to expand on what they already know.

~Kristen Haase, Third- Through Fifth-Grade English Development Teacher

Introduction

What is one of the best ways to get people talking? Get them talking about themselves. People enjoy talking about their families, their interests, and their daily lives. Why? It makes them feel good. It is estimated that on average, people spend 60% of conversations talking about themselves—and this figure jumps to 80% when communicating via social media platforms such as Twitter or Facebook (Naaman et al., 2010). Since people are doing this already, let's get our students to talk more about themselves, their families, and their interests using elevated language. Let's talk about how and when we can make that happen.

Description

Teachers connect with their students daily. These interactions are some of the most meaningful and impactful conversations in a student's day. They are one-on-one, and the student feels important and valued. These interactions offer some of the best teaching opportunities, and they can happen inside and outside of the instructional classroom. We can make the most out of them by using substitutionary language!

Rationale

What do students need to know? By the end of their elementary career, students need to be able to read complex text and write using a wide repertoire of sentence structures and academic vocabulary. In addition, students need to be able to write multiple sentences on a topic to form paragraphs and essays.

What's the challenge? Research shows that listening comprehension skills are stronger than reading comprehension skills in younger learners (Stricht & James, 1984). The exposure to complex sentence structure and academic vocabulary is often found in texts, not through social conversations. However, if students are not exposed to complex sentence structure and elevated language before they are expected to read complex text and write using these structures and vocabulary, they may struggle to complete these tasks.

What does the strategy offer? This strategy offers ideas on how to use substitutionary language during everyday conversations. Spoken discourse involves speaking multiple sentences around a theme. We can capitalize on these conversations when we choose themes that are important to students. Seizing every opportunity to build our students' vocabulary is paramount, and these impromptu conversations offer an opportunity to insert elevated language into topics about which the students already have a fair amount of background knowledge. Some might argue, "Won't I sound pretentious and pompous?" Our objective is to expand all students' vocabularies. For some students, a school setting is the only place they will be exposed to robust, elevated language. When teachers model elevated language, they are providing equity to their students.

Ideas in Action

When are some possible times to use elevated language at the discourse level?

- In the morning, as students are entering the classroom
- Before, during, or after lunch
- At the end of the day, as students are packing up to leave the building
- During transitions throughout the day

At the beginning of the year, Kristen creates a simple chart that helps her keep track of her students' interests. Kristen collects this data through informal conversations as well as having students discuss their weekends (this can be done orally or in writing). While the focus of this book is bolstering student language through oral, strategic modeling, teachers can also gain information through narrative writing, dialogue journals, and questionnaires.

During the year, Kristen uses a chart similar to the one shown. As she learns more about her students, she adds details to the "Interests" section.

Kristen adds more words and phrases to the chart, which provides her with words she can use while speaking with the students. The authors suggest teachers continue to ask their students about their interests. Conversing with students about their interests will give you the background knowledge needed to expand your questioning.

Student Name	Interests	Words and Phrases Other important information
Kristen	anime	creations, drawings, Japanese

Some teachers may say "I don't know a lot about some of their interests." Here is an opportunity for growth. Similar to Strategy # 2, you start gradually. A word here and there. In addition, educate yourself a little on the topic. If it's a video game, play it, or watch a YouTube video about it. Make a game out of it for yourself. Kristen's students are impressed when she says she plays *Fortnite*. She and her students have great conversations about it. When they say words like "kill," she says, "Let's use the word 'eliminate' instead." After that quick, simple directive, she notices them using the word "eliminate." Her teaching points really stick because they already know all about the game. You are not asking them to learn new material *and* learn new vocabulary. That is why this strategy is so important.

In addition, some teachers might say "Will using elevated language during these social interactions inhibit my ability to connect with my students?" Think of the example when Kristen speaks to her students about *Fortnite*. They are so thrilled their teachers have taken interest in one of their favorite pastimes, they cannot wait to tell her about their latest game. Since they know enough about the game, Kristen can easily use substitutionary language. In turn, since they are experts in the game, they already have the background knowledge to be successful in understanding the handful of words she chooses to substitute.

Think back to the Benevolent Conspiracy in Chapter 1. If we are not allowing our students the opportunity to grow because we think they will not understand us or want to interact with us, we are missing an opportunity to bolster their vocabulary. Therefore, we must seize on every opportunity daily.

The Tale of Two Teachers

Here are two samples of a 20-second conversation teachers may have with students who enjoy watching football. Read the conversations below. Then complete the compare-and-contrast chart based on your observations.

Teacher A

Teacher: Did you see the Cowboys' game on Sunday?
Student: Yeah.
Teacher: Did you see the great catch?
Student: Which one?
Teacher: The one that Lamb made.
Student: Yeah.

Teacher B

Teacher: Did you view the Cowboys' game on Sunday evening?
Student: Yeah.
Teacher: Did you witness the phenomenal catch by the wide receiver in the back of the end zone toward the end of the game? If so, what was your perspective?
Student: Yeah, Lamb really made a great grab.
Teacher: In addition, Dak (the quarterback) propelled a perfect spiral that landed right in his outstretched hands.

Reflection Questions

Teacher A	Same	Teacher B

Below are the authors' comparisons:

Teacher A	Same	Teacher B
• Tier 1 vocabulary ○ see ○ catch ○ game ○ great • Simple sentences • Vague language ○ On Sunday	• Topic • Teacher and student having a conversation • Teacher is keeping the conversation going • Yes/no questions	• Tier 2 and 3 vocabulary ○ witness ○ view ○ propelled ○ phenomenal ○ spiral • Expanded sentences • Complex sentences • Precise language ○ on Sunday evening • Asked an open-ended question

Serendipitous conversations throughout the day are all opportunities for bolstering discourse through strategic modeling. This strategy is especially effective when the teacher builds on the interests of the students. As veteran teachers, we know how much is on your plate. We do not want to add more. Most likely, you are already engaging your students in conversations. We just want you to be mindful of this opportunity. After you know the students' interests, substitutionary language will happen organically. You may need to do a little research on topics you have little familiarity with; however, most of their interests are topics about which you will have some background knowledge.

Students need to build on one another's ideas during conversations, which is a skill that sets them up for success when they present arguments. A key component of building discourse during conversations is keeping the conversation going. Teachers can model this by asking follow-up questions like Teacher B did in the example conversation.

Types of Questions	Question Starters
Yes/No	Did you . . . ? Do you like . . . ?
One-Word/Short-Phrase Responses	Where did you . . . ? What did you . . . ?
Longer Responses	Why did you . . . ? How did you . . . ?

It is important to keep in mind the level of English proficiency of your students. Using yes/no questions will help build their vocabulary and comprehension. Higher-order questions can be asked of your beginning English learners; however, they will need to be scaffolded. This can be done by using visuals and gesturing.

With that being said, do not shy away from having conversations with your beginning ELs. Using elevated language with these students needs to be carefully monitored. Remember, ELs just entering the country and your classrooms will need time to acquire language. Once students develop a working vocabulary, you can build off the words they know.

Tips for ELs

They Say It, We Say It

Janet Purcell, ESL teacher and ESL college instructor, capitalizes on the visual benefits of videos in building her students' background knowledge while improving their fluency and academic vocabulary. Janet created a strategy she calls They Say It, We Say It. She begins by carefully choosing a video that contains background knowledge on the subject to be taught.

After describing the process to the students and posting it on the board, the video is played for the *first* time. Then students carefully listen to the narration. After the viewing, new concepts and vocabulary are explained.

In the *second* viewing of the video, Janet mutes the sound and narrates the video herself. In this way, she is able to simplify language if necessary and repeat and clarify targeted vocabulary. In addition, Janet pauses the film at strategic points to provide more information on the topic, using key vocabulary. She also stresses the importance of repetition as a key factor in language learning. Janet emphasizes, "Students need building blocks for their language, one of which is vocabulary. Each subject has its own specialized vocabulary which needs to be clearly explained so that students will increase their academic vocabulary (CALP)" (Cummins, 1979). She also stresses the importance of repetition as a key factor in vocabulary and language learning. Most of the vocabulary words will later be practiced either through crossword puzzle homework or games played in the classroom or on the student tablets.

The video is played for a *third* time, and each student is assigned a segment to narrate independently. The students then are given time to write their script for their segment of the narration. The teacher is available for assistance and then pronunciation and fluency help when the student begins to orally practice his/her narration.

After students begin to feel confident with their narration segment, the *fourth* and future playing of the video is segmentally narrated by the students.

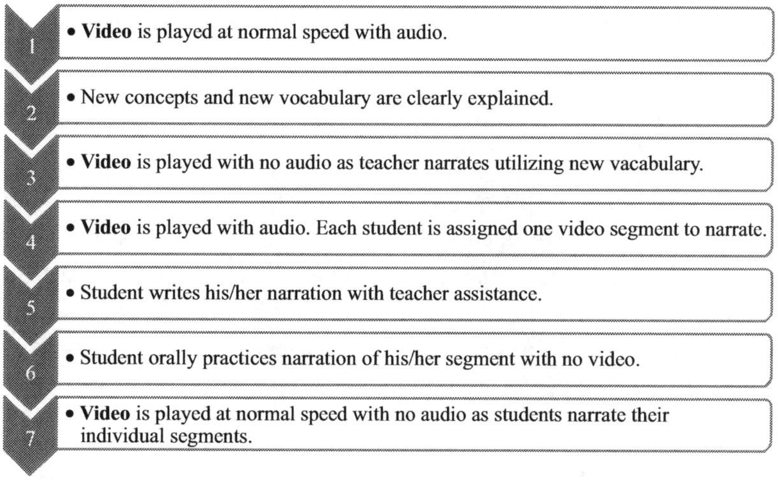

Figure 4j.1 Purcell's They Say It, We Say It Graphic

This final exercise combines fluency, academic vocabulary, and pronunciation practice in a topic that is new to the student. Review of the final exercise can be practiced at the beginning of the next class or two to reinforce the students' confidence in his/her oral skills.

References

Cummins, J. (1979). *Cognitive/academic language proficiency, linguistic interdependence, the optimum age question and some other matters*. Working Papers on Bilingualism, No. 19, 121–129.

Naaman, M., Boase, J., & Lai, C. H. (2010). *Is it really about me? Message content in social awareness streams*. Rutgers University, School of Communication and Information 4 Huntington St.

Stricht, T. G., & James, J. H. (1984). Listening and reading. In P. D. Pearson, R. Barr, M. L. Kamil, & P. Mosenthal (Eds.), *Handbook of reading research* (Vol. 1, pp. 293–317). Longman.

Strategy #11: Modeling Discourse to Address the Common Core Standards

Strategy Focus

Understanding the language of the Common Core Standards including standardized tests and exams can be challenging for many students, as many of the terms are abstract and used most often in an academic setting. Words such as "explain," "summarize," "compare," "contrast," and "analyze" can be reinforced to students in a variety of contexts when teachers deliberately use the principle of substitutionary language.

Strategy #11: Modeling Discourse to Address the Common Core Standards

Introduction

Standards, standards, standards. What are administrators looking for when they visit your classrooms and watch your lessons? We can bet that the word "standard" will come up. What standard are you addressing? How are you addressing the standard? How do you know if the students have mastered the standard? The list could go on and on.

Consider the following standards: summarizing, comparing, contrasting, stating one's opinion and giving supporting reasons, providing arguments, identifying the main idea and key details, and narrating. Most of these skills involve the creation of spoken or written discourse around a topic. So how do we learn these skills? While writing certainly is one way, it is not the only way. In Strategy #10, the authors stressed the importance of seizing opportunities to model for students how to expand on their ideas, interests, and spontaneous conversations. In this chapter, the authors build upon the strategies in Chapter 10. If students have been exposed to the concepts in areas that are very familiar to them, teachers can then shift these strategic modeling opportunities to the academic topics and texts connected to the rigorous standards. By engaging students in discourse, utilizing the standards, we can help them gain the valuable repetition they need with these types of skills.

Description

This strategy incorporates oral language and the Common Core standards. In order to implement this strategy, teachers will need to have a solid understanding of the academic standards. They will use their knowledge of the standards to seize on previously missed opportunities. Such opportunities may present themselves in morning meetings, during impromptu conversations throughout the instructional day, or at other times during the school day.

Rationale

What do students need to know? Understanding the academic core standards is crucial for students to be successful at any grade level. Students need to be able to perform at a proficient level in the domains of speaking, listening, reading, and writing. In addition, they need to demonstrate an understanding of content area standards in which the four domains mentioned are intertwined.

What's the challenge? By the time elementary students enter the intermediate grades, speaking and listening standards become secondary. In the authors' experience, they may not be addressed with the same fidelity as the reading and writing standards. As a result, the students' first exposure to the rigorous academic standards is during reading and writing instruction. In their 2014 article "Speaking and Listening in Content Area Learning," Douglas Fisher and Nancy Frey advise teachers to attend to the increased demands of the Speaking and Listening domains. While the students need to be able to read on grade level in order to be proficient, many students would benefit from discussing, answering questions, summarizing, presenting arguments, and engaging in the other uses of language orally before they are asked to address them in their reading and writing.

What does the strategy offer? This strategy offers ideas for addressing the standards outside the reading and writing classroom. Using the language of the standards outside of the instructional classroom will allow the students to become more familiar with the language and organization of the standards. Let's explore more!

Ideas in Action

> *As a teenage girl, I remember asking my parents if I could get a car. I remember my father, who is a retired attorney, telling me to come back when I had formulated my opinion, and strengthened my argument with facts. He said be ready to refute any argument he might have with my opinion.*
>
> *I needed to do this more than once growing up; however, this helped me throughout my adult life. Think about what a valuable skill this is in all walks of life. Now, think about the possibilities for our students if they are asked to do more than just state their opinions.*
>
> *~Kristen Haase*

In order to be college and career ready, students must be proficient in the standards. Young students, left to their own, may not elaborate on their thoughts and ideas but rather give little information on a topic. How do we expect students to elaborate on complex ideas related to the standards in their writing if they have not had the opportunity to do so in their speaking?

Reflection Activity

1. Before we get started, brainstorm a few standards from your curriculum and write them in the space below. For this activity, choose reading and writing standards. You could complete this activity on your own, with a colleague(s) in other grade levels, or in grade-level teams. Brainstorm standards you feel are most important for the students to know.

Standard 1 ____
Standard 2 ____
Standard 3 ____

Now, let's take a look at how we can address those standards orally. In order to provide an example, we chose a Common Core ELA literature standard and examined it across grade levels. Consider the opinion/persuasive/argumentative writing standard across the grade levels.

Kindergarten

CCSS.ELA-LITERACY.W.K.3
Use a combination of drawing, dictating, and writing to narrate a single event or several loosely linked events, tell about the events in the order in which they occurred, and provide a reaction to what happened.

First Grade

CCSS.ELA-LITERACY.W.1.1
Write opinion pieces in which they introduce the topic or name the book they are writing about, state an opinion, supply a reason for the opinion, and provide some sense of closure.

Second Grade

CCSS.ELA-LITERACY.W.2.1
Write opinion pieces in which they introduce the topic or book they are writing about, state an opinion, supply reasons that support the opinion, use linking words (e.g., *because, and, also*) to connect opinion and reasons, and provide a concluding statement or section.

Third Grade

CCSS.ELA-LITERACY.W.3.1.A
Introduce the topic or text they are writing about, state an opinion, and create an organizational structure that lists reasons.
CCSS.ELA-LITERACY.W.3.1.B
Provide reasons that support the opinion.
CCSS.ELA-LITERACY.W.3.1.B
Provide reasons that support the opinion.
CCSS.ELA-LITERACY.W.3.1.C
Use linking words and phrases (e.g., *because, therefore, since, for example*) to connect opinion and reasons.
CCSS.ELA-LITERACY.W.3.1.D
Provide a concluding statement or section.

Fourth Grade

CCSS.ELA-LITERACY.W.4.1.A
Introduce a topic or text clearly, state an opinion, and create an organizational structure in which related ideas are grouped to support the writer's purpose.
CCSS.ELA-LITERACY.W.4.1.B
Provide reasons that are supported by facts and details.
CCSS.ELA-LITERACY.W.4.1.C
Link opinion and reasons using words and phrases (e.g., *for instance, in order to, in addition*).
CCSS.ELA-LITERACY.W.4.1.D
Provide a concluding statement or section related to the opinion presented.

Fifth Grade

CCSS.ELA-LITERACY.W.5.1
Write opinion pieces on topics or texts, supporting a point of view with reasons and information.
CCSS.ELA-LITERACY.W.5.1.A
Introduce a topic or text clearly, state an opinion, and create an organizational structure in which ideas are logically grouped to support the writer's purpose.
CCSS.ELA-LITERACY.W.5.1.B
Provide logically ordered reasons that are supported by facts and details.

CCSS.ELA-LITERACY.W.5.1.C
Link opinion and reasons using words, phrases, and clauses (e.g., *consequently, specifically*).
CCSS.ELA-LITERACY.W.5.1.D
Provide a concluding statement or section related to the opinion presented.

2. Now, let's take a moment to reflect on these standards. What do you notice? How are they the same? How are they different? What do students need to know?

 ____
 ____
 ____
 ____

3. List common words or phrases used across the standards.

 ____
 ____

4. In what ways could you model these standards outside of reading and writing instruction?

 ____
 ____
 ____

Let's explore some of the ways you could use strategic modeling through teacher talk while addressing the standards throughout the day.

Oral Scrimmages

We know the language demands increase quickly as students move from one grade to the next. Many of the Common Core State Standards, as they develop across grade levels, require students to move from producing single sentences to discourse in the form of paragraphs and essays. Students are asked to use language to describe, narrate, explain, inform, and argue, just to mention a few functions. For example, first graders are asked to state their opinion with a supporting reason in the form of a sentence, "My favorite season is winter because I like to make snow angels." While the language demands ask students to write a few sentences on a topic in the primary grades, the demands change to discourse in the upper elementary grades. Among the skills fifth- and sixth-grade students are asked to master are:

- Write arguments to support claims with clear reasons and relevant evidence
- Introduce a topic clearly and group related information in paragraphs
- Compare two or more characters
- Develop a topic with facts, definitions, concrete details, quotations, or other information and examples related to the topic

In order to meet the rigorous writing demands of the Common Core Standards, we need to revise our typical progression of activities leading up to students' writing of their final product. We know that in order for students to acquire language at the word, sentence, or discourse level, many exposures are needed to become familiar with the vocabulary, sentence syntax, transition words, and organizational structures.

Carmen incorporated a practice with her students she calls "oral scrimmages" to underscore the importance of practicing both listening to and talking through academic discourse. Just as athletes on a sports team engage in many scrimmages to hone the skills they need before the big game, our students need the same when it comes to organizing their discourse. The first diagram shows the typical progression of activities that lead up to a student's written product. In many classrooms, students are often afforded an opportunity to discuss their ideas with a peer. Then students organize their thoughts in a web or graphic organizer. Finally, the student writes the final essay, oftentimes through a series of rough drafts. This typical process is not without its problems.

There are two problems inherent in the typical progression of discourse writing activities. First, although the use of a graphic organizer is an appropriate scaffold for learners new to discourse writing, it may need to be removed depending on the writing assignment or when students become adept at organizing their own thoughts. Continuing to use graphic organizers without oral rehearsals or "oral scrimmages" creates a dependency on them. Instead of making endless revisions because of missing evidence or rationales, students refine their thinking at a much faster rate orally. "Oral scrimmages" allow students to grow their thinking and discourse organizational skills exponentially because they are temporarily unencumbered with writing. In this way students gain valuable practice in the skills they truly need.

Second, writing and typing on a keyboard are both laborious processes for most elementary-aged students. While this affords them much practice

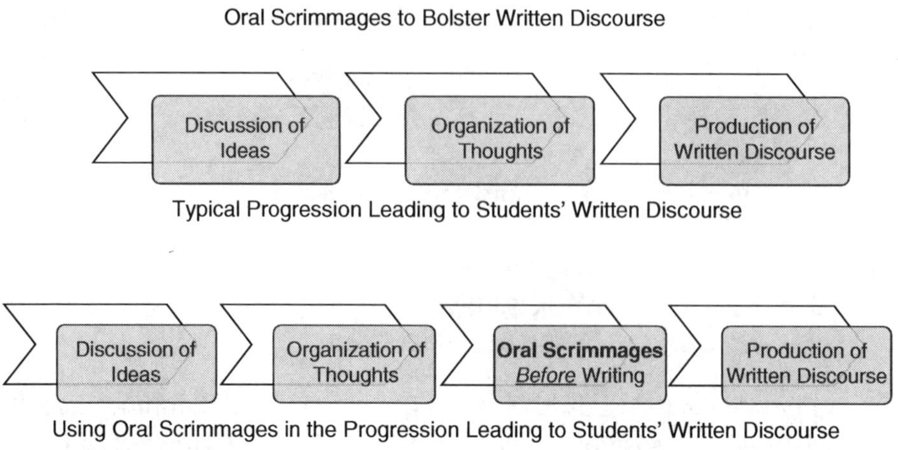

Figure 4k.1 Oral Scrimmages

with handwriting and typing, the greater need is practice in formulating and organizing their thoughts. Writing and typing, in many cases, slow the thinking process down. As a result, very little time is left for the higher-order thinking needed for meeting the rigor of the standards. Allowing students opportunities to engage in oral scrimmages enables them to get closer to the final product with fewer time-consuming edits and rough drafts.

Teachers should model this type of oral discourse for their students prior to the start of students' writing and serendipitously as occasions arise throughout the school day. Furthermore, students should work in cooperative learning groups to take turns talking through their thinking and organization of writing, just as they would write it. Through many scrimmages, our students will have gained the necessary practice they need for the "big game," their essays.

"Lightening the Cognitive Load Through Exposure to Discourse"

As students progress through elementary school, they will be expected to develop their background knowledge on a variety of academic topics and develop the discourse skills in order to meet the rigorous Common Core Standards. For many students, starting and organizing discourse is challenging. The process of organizing their thoughts and ideas is stretched out over days and sometimes weeks. Students sometimes struggle to make the connections between their note-taking and the final organization of those notes into discourse. Through oral scrimmages and strategic modeling of discourse, teachers can help familiarize students with the organization of thoughts as they relate to the standards. When students are faced with the double challenge of unknown topics and organizing their thoughts into discourse, academic tasks can be daunting. The following chart shows how we can lighten the cognitive load for students through repetitive modeling of discourse in order to create familiarity.

Quadrant 1	**Quadrant 3**
Familiar With Discourse & Topic • Student possesses much background knowledge on the topic • Student is familiar with the vocabulary associated with the topic • Student is able to articulate thoughts through discourse	Unfamiliar With Discourse/ Familiar With Topic • Student possesses background knowledge on the topic • Student is familiar with the vocabulary associated with the topic • Student is unable to articulate thoughts though discourse
Quadrant 2	**Quadrant 4**
Familiar With Discourse/ Unfamiliar With Topic • Student does not possess much background knowledge on the topic • Students is unfamiliar with much of the vocabulary around the topic • Student is able to articulate thoughts through discourse	Unfamiliar With Discourse & Topic • Student does not possess background knowledge on the topic • Student is unfamiliar with the vocabulary associated with the topic • Student is unable to articulate thoughts though discourse

One opportunity to lighten the load is when you hear a student state an opinion. For example, a few years ago, Kristen had a few intermediate elementary Level 3 ELs who were adamant about not wanting to wear uniforms. Some of the comments she heard were, "It is not fair, Miss." "Other schools don't have to." Her response was, "I hear you. Now what are your reasons?" Blank stares followed. After a few moments of silence, someone piped up. "We just don't want to wear them." To this, she replied, "OK, but you are going to have to do better than that if you want to *convince* people. This decision is made by district leaders, so you will need some *strong arguments* to support this *opinion*. You are also going to have to *persuade* people to change

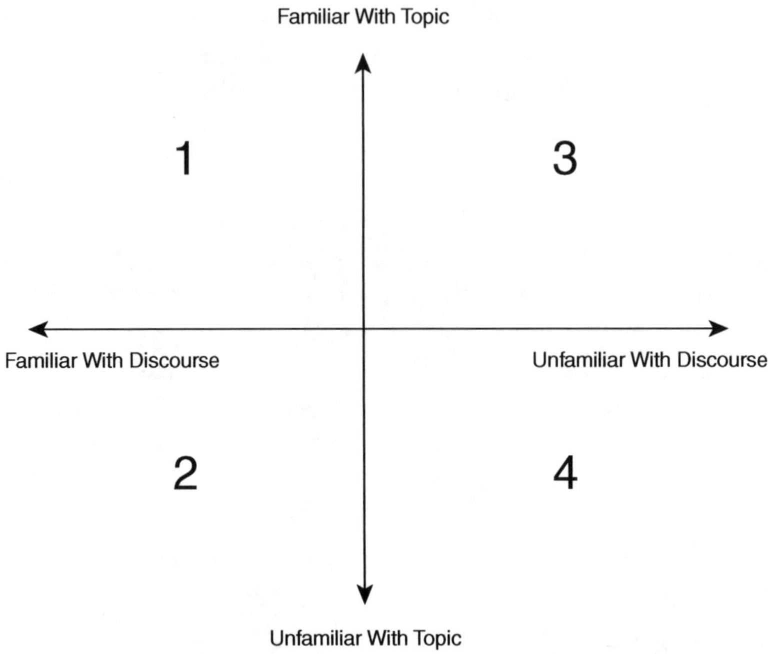

Figure 4k.2 Lightening Students' Cognitive Load Through Exposure to Discourse (Copyright Haase and Rowe)

the *policy*. Lastly, you need to be prepared to hear the other side and *refute* their *reasons*. Let me show you how we do this."

***A Tip for ELs: Notice how she uses the language of the standards in this exchange. Level 3 students can comprehend her because she uses the words in context, and students have a good understanding of the topic they are discussing.

Reflection Question

1. Consider the scenario involving Kristen's students and their desire to not wear uniforms. With respect to (1) familiarity with the topic and (2) familiarity with discourse, plot Kristen's students in the most appropriate coordinate.

Connecting to the Standards Through Impromptu Modeling

The following chart shows an example of how teachers can use a framework for opinion discourse.

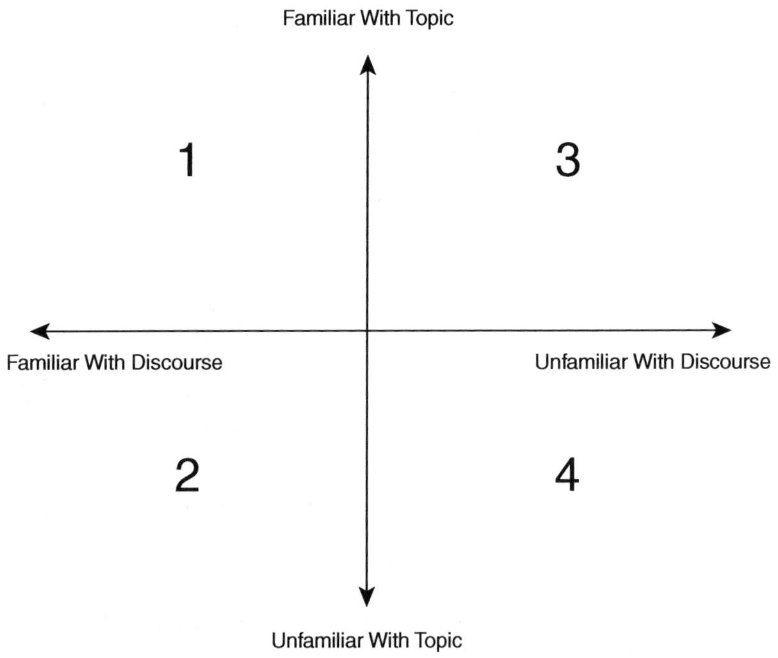

Figure 4k.3 Lightening Students' Cognitive Load Through Exposure to Discourse (Copyright Haase and Rowe)

Opinion Statement
Reason 1
Persuasion 1
Argument Against
Reason 2
Persuasion 2
Argument Against
Concluding Statement

Framework for Opinion Discourse

While the chart is modeled on the fifth-grade standard of opinion writing, it could be modified for any grade level. Kristen uses this model when students make oral opinion statements. Questioning and prompting are key during such exchanges. The more you incorporate the language of the standards in your exchanges, the more the students will become familiar with that language.

Here is a conversation with a second grader.

Kristen: How was your weekend?
Student: Good. (Opinion Statement)

Kristen: So, in your opinion, your weekend was good. Tell me one reason it was good.

Student: We went to the park. (Reason 1)

Kristen: Going to the park sounds quite enjoyable. What did you do at the park?

Student: My brother and I played tag. (Evidence that goes with reason 1 that supports the opinion)

Kristen: What do you like about playing tag?

Student: I love chasing my brother. ("Because" statement to support reason)

Kristen: So let's summarize. One reason your weekend was good is because you went to the park. You played tag with your brother because you love chasing your brother. That is one reason why your weekend was good. (Teacher models entire summary)

This exchange probably lasted a minute. Notice how you could expand on this if you had more time. You could elicit another reason and use the same questioning and prompting techniques.

***A Tip for ELs: A word of caution with using this strategy with ELs. If your goal is to familiarize students with the standards, consider using common words and phrases at first. Using too many academic terms and too much elevated language could cause confusion and derail you from your goal.

Put It Into Practice

1. Create a mock conversation asking about a student's weekend. Reference the opinion standards suggested for the grade level you teach. You can use Kristen's Framework for Opinion Discourse, or you can create one of your own. We've started the dialog for you.

Strategic Modeling of Opinion Discourse Teacher: How was your weekend? Student: ______________ (Opinion Statement)

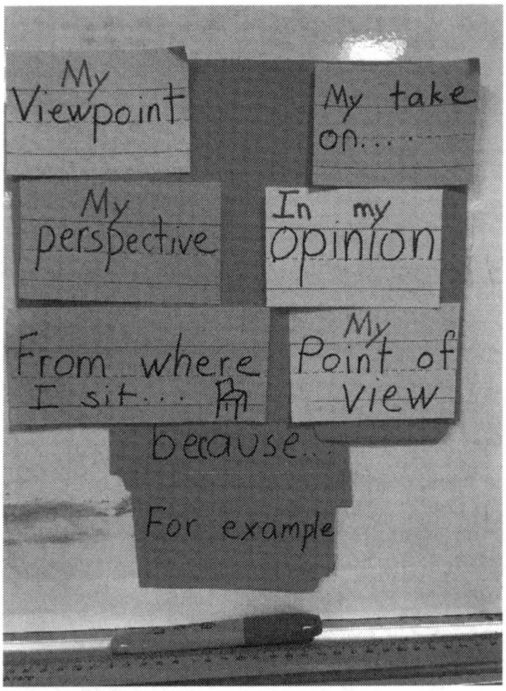

Figure 4k.4 Substitutionary Language for Stating One's Opinion

Tips for Working With ELs

Stating Your Opinion

Jeanne Oakes and Yara Graupera, elementary ESL teachers, provided their first-grade students with alternative ways of stating their opinions. The poster in Figure 4k.4 earned a prominent place near the carpet where children gather for morning meetings. Every morning over the course of a week, the students were asked to give their viewpoint on a variety of topics. "What's your favorite season and why?" and "Should students be required to wear uniforms?" were among the prompts. To aid teachers and students in using a variety of ways to express their opinions, the poster reminded everyone of their options.

Reference

Fisher, D., & Frey, N. (2014). Speaking and listening in content area learning. *The Reading Teacher*, *68*(1).

Strategy #12: Emphasizing Character Traits and Theme

Strategy Focus

Possessing a broad vocabulary is essential for students when discussing character traits and themes found in literature in the ELA classroom. In this strategy, teachers will be equipped with ideas for modeling and reinforcing, throughout the day, the vocabulary associated with the character traits and themes found in literature in ways that connect to students personally.

Strategy #12: Emphasizing Character Traits and Theme

Introduction

Children learn character traits implicitly early in life. Caregivers of young children often hear the children say words like "mean," "tall," and "nice" when describing their peers. As teachers of elementary-aged students, we often hear our students using these same adjectives to describe characters in books they hear or read. As students advance in their academic careers, these common words are no longer acceptable if they are to be successful in academic settings.

Description

Students at all grade levels learn about story elements that are key features of studying literature. While kindergartners begin their study by learning about characters, setting, and major events of a story, our upper elementary students determine the theme from details in the story, including how characters in a story respond to challenges. In order to discuss the theme, or the underlying message about life that the author is trying to convey, students will need a knowledge of the characters, in particular their character traits.

Rationale

What do students need to know? Modeling character traits and themes is a powerful strategy because it inherently holds relevance for every one of us in analyzing not only characters in literature but also ourselves. We all possess positive and negative character traits. As we expose students to this vocabulary, they learn the precise language needed in ELA and in life.

What's the challenge? In most literature, we, the readers or listeners, are left to make inferences about what specific traits the characters display based on their words, actions, thoughts, and emotions. Sometimes the author will give us insights into the characters' personality through their motives for doing or not doing something. So how, then, will students learn the names of the wide array of character traits when they are not always explicitly mentioned in texts?

What does the strategy offer? This strategy offers scores of opportunities to teach character traits by specifically naming both the positive and negative ones as they present themselves during the school day. The strategy also offers insights on how to infuse the topic throughout the day as well as through the school year.

Ideas in Action

Character Trait Man

Developing a robust vocabulary is essential in academia. This is no less true in the English language arts classroom. From the time young learners begin school in kindergarten, they are introduced to the basic story elements. As they progress through elementary school, the expectations of their knowledge of literature and their ability to describe and analyze characters grow. The basic vocabulary used in social situations to describe character traits most often does not provide nuanced meanings or appropriate register required by the standards. Carmen illustrates this point through the following anecdote:

While working with a group of fifth-grade students reading a novel, they encountered the word "meticulous,' to describe one of the main characters. Based on what they knew about the character, Carmen asked students to make an inference about the meaning of the word "meticulous." "It means someone who's a 'neat freak,' " quipped a student. She affirmed the student's inference and went on to explain that "neat freak" is a more informal term, whereas "meticulous" is more formal.

Carmen made a mental note to intentionally use the word "meticulous" with her students. The following day, they continued their discussion of the main character. She asked if her students remembered the new word for "neat freak." They recalled the discussion, but no one could remember the word "meticulous." It was then and there that the idea for Character Trait Man was born. She knew that as a class, they needed a way to access the newly learned vocabulary. Following is the larger-than-life two-sided Character Trait Man, displaying both positive and negative traits.

Carmen printed out the word "meticulous," and a discussion ensued over which side of Character Trait Man the new word should be added. A conundrum ensued. "Is meticulous a positive trait or a negative one?" we asked. The students saw evidence in the book that this trait helped the character to organize himself and his belongings, leading to effective study habits . . . that was

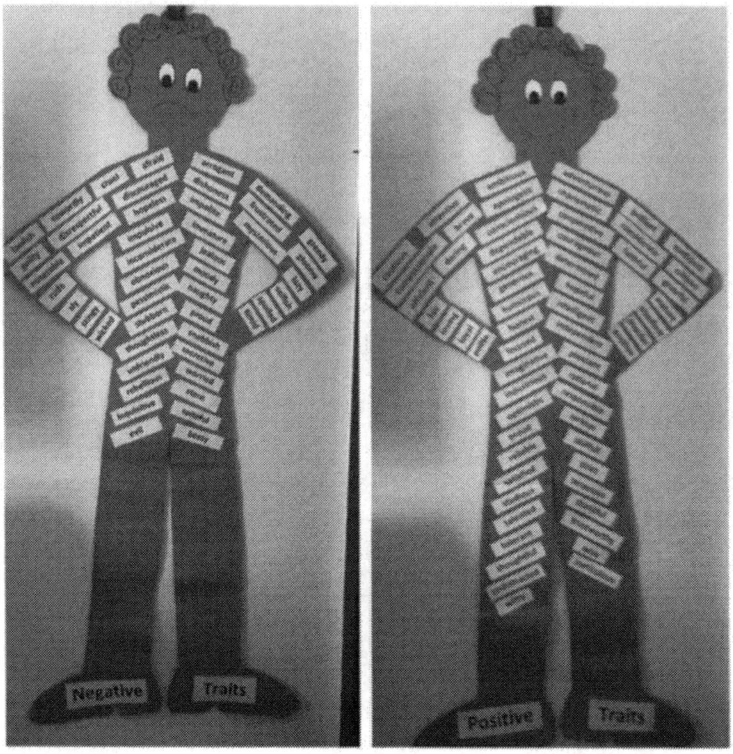

Figure 4I.1 Character Trait Man

positive. However, the students also witnessed the character's obsession with maintaining a meticulous appearance, leading to great distraction and anger when his clothes became soiled while he walked to school. In the end, the students decided that the trait could be both positive and negative, two sides of the same coin, and added to both sides of Character Trait Man.

When creating a Character Trait Man chart, be sure to work together with your students to decide on which words will be added and where. Carmen's chart began with one word, and then she and her students added to it daily or weekly. The words were alphabetized and shifted as needed. Interestingly, Carmen notes, "My students knew exactly where each word was located because we regularly accessed the chart when engaging in literature texts."

Classroom teacher Amanda Aikens, commented on the effectiveness of Character Trait Man to serve as a reminder to teachers and students alike to use elevated language. "Within days, students were no longer using 'happy,' 'sad,' 'nice,' and 'mean' to describe characters. All of a sudden, we heard words such as 'pessimistic,' 'dependable,' 'loyal,' and 'humble'" (A. Aikens, personal communication, May 15, 2022).

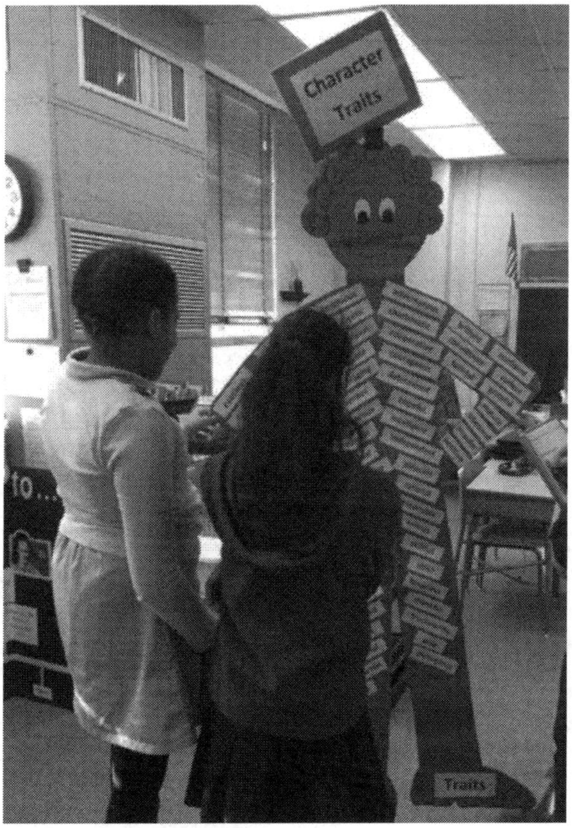

Figure 4I.2 Character Trait Man in Action

"Three Positives and a Negative"

A great extension for intermediate students is to ask them to complete a "Three Positives and a Negative" character analysis organizer. When reading literature, routinely ask them to analyze the main character and/or characters with respect to three positives and one negative character trait and evidence from the text as a rationale for why they chose each trait. Using Character Trait Man as a reference, Carmen's students were faithfully able to access the elevated academic character traits.

The Use of Songs in the Classroom

The use of songs in the classroom is often overlooked, and yet lyrics set to music can be highly motivating and relevant for our students. In addition, songs provide a completely oral medium for students. Many stories have been set to music and provide excellent opportunities for character analysis and inferring themes. Reading may be abstract for budding learners, and songs often provide access to literary skills through a common media replete with musical elements. Perhaps one of the greatest rationales for using songs in the classroom is that it provides equal access for all students, proficient and struggling readers alike. The chart that follows provides guidance for teachers who want to implement songs when teaching themes.

Step 1	Pick a song that is appropriate for the age group of your students. Considerations: • Songs with a storyline are preferable • Songs with a theme that aligns to literature being taught • Consider varied tempo, pitch, dynamics, and instrumentation
Step 2	Allow students to listen to the song in its entirety
Step 3	Ask questions that all students could respond to: • How did the song make you feel? • In your opinion, was it a happy song, a sad song . . .?
Step 4	Allow students to listen to the song a second time, specifically listening for one or more of the following: • Were there repetitive phrases? • How do you think the person singing feels? • How did the instruments contribute to the mood of the song?
Step 5	Discuss the following open-ended prompts: • What character traits does the singer possess? Provide evidence to support your opinion. • What is the overall theme of the song? Provide evidence to support your opinion.

An Extension to This Activity

Providing students with background knowledge on the songwriter's life and motive for writing the song can inspire students to deeply analyze songs and literature. By doing this, you have given your students a lifelong skill, since they will most likely continue to listen to music throughout their lives. Allow your students to select a song of their choice to analyze or research. In addition, teachers could ask their students to compare and contrast songs by the same artists. Are there common themes among the artist's songs? Are there similar details in the artist's songs?

Reflection Activity

1. When introducing this activity, choose a song with a clear storyline that is appropriate for your students. Use the chart that follows to work through the questions you will ask of your students.

Step 1	Song Title:
Step 2	Allow students to listen to the song in its entirety.
Step 3	Question/s related to the singer's emotions:
Step 4	Allow students to listen to the song a second time. Focus questions:
Step 5	Open-ended prompt:

Tips for Working With ELs

In order for ELs to understand literature standards involving themes and character traits, it is important to build background knowledge. ELs are rich with personal experiences, so it is imperative we build on them. When the students are learning about themes and character traits, Kristen often likes to start by using her students' own lives as examples. One way to do this is to connect to the students' lives. Kristen notes two themes that pertain to her students' lives: courage and perseverance. Orally, she talks about the details in their lives that go along with these two themes. Leaving their home countries, learning a new language, the exhaustion that comes with hearing English every day. Then we talk about what kinds of words describe the students and their actions. We come up with words and phrases like "brave," "fearless," "persistent," "never giving up," "having hope."

She then creates an anchor chart in her room like the one that follows. This chart serves numerous purposes. First and foremost, it gives the students a sense of pride and accomplishment. Second, it serves as a reference. Kristen tells the students all of these characteristics, themes, and actions transfer to their reading. When students encounter characters with similar traits in a book they are reading or listening to, they can connect with the characters in order to better understand the characters and their actions. It is imperative that they are able to make connections between their own lives and what they are learning in the classroom.

The chart also provides the opportunity for students to understand themes in literature as well as in life. Common themes start to prevail when students are able to see similar character traits relating to the same themes.

Theme	Students	Character Traits	Actions
Perseverance	Francisco	bold, stubborn, committed, persistent	• Struggling to read and write in English • Asking for help • Coming to school every day
Courage	Abedi	brave, fearless, leader	• Leaving family behind in Africa • Getting on an airplane • Walking into school on the first day knowing not a word of English

Long after the unit on theme and character traits is over, her students are still talking about them. As a ticket out the door or exit ticket, Kristen will often say the theme of the day was "perseverance" and ask the students for examples. Students will answer, "We worked hard on our writing. We asked questions when we didn't understand." Teachers can also have students talk about actions that happened in class that day and come up with a common theme.

Other situations in the students' lives can generate discussion centered around themes. Teachers can ask what the theme of their weekend was. If they have trouble, teachers can ask them to tell them the details of their weekend. As a result, themes often develop as they are giving their details.

When teachers speak with their students about themes and character traits, they can learn more about their students and their families, which helps them to form meaningful relationships. In addition, this is an opportunity to maximize what they have accomplished in their young lives.

Common Themes in Children's Literature

Courage	Kindness
Perseverance	Honesty
Preparedness	Friendship
Cooperation	Acceptance
Resourcefulness	Compassion

Highlighting a Theme of the Week or Day

Teachers can further highlight specific themes by featuring one each day or week. Here is an example of an anchor chart you can create and post in your classroom. Notice the theme is listed along with examples of actions that exemplify that theme, as well as character traits. A column is available for teachers to recognize students who demonstrate the theme.

Theme of the Day/Week	Actions that Contribute to the Theme	Students	Character Traits
Cooperation	• Reading a book together • Encouraging others to do their part • Listening to others ideas	Student A Student B Student C	patient, helpful, attentive, cooperative appreciative, encouraging

Please note: When working with ELs, teachers should build gradually on their current vocabulary. When discussing theme and character traits:

1. Focus on one or two themes to start. Define the themes using comprehensible input, words they will understand that may be slightly above their current language level.
2. Select a few character traits that go with that theme.
3. Define those character traits using comprehensible input.
4. Relate the character traits to the students in your classroom before introducing character traits in literature.

5

Building a Schoolwide Culture of Substitutionary Language

How Can We Enlist the Help of All School Staff?

- Ongoing professional development
- Time for teacher reflection and collaboration
- Data collection and inspection

When teachers and administrators are committed to these goals, each individual teacher's efforts are exponentially increased as the principle of substitutionary language is implemented across grade levels and subject areas as a schoolwide culture.

Introduction

One teacher who seizes opportunities to model elevated language for his or her students can have a great impact on that group of students. However, imagine the impact if all teachers at every grade level, all content areas, and all staff within a building were implementing elevated language in their speech throughout the day. In doing so, the school would increase the likelihood of expanding its students' vocabularies and language through repetition.

Reading expert Shanahan (2005) supported the importance of repetition:

> the most effective direct instruction in vocabulary helps children gain deep understanding of word meanings (much more than simple dictionary definitions); requires plenty of reading, writing, talking, and

DOI: 10.4324/9781003295716-6

listening; emphasizes the interconnections among words and word meanings and the connections of words to children's own experiences; and provides abundant ongoing review and repetition.

(p. 30)

Kinsella (2018) acknowledged that if students are to achieve the Common Core State Standards (CCSS, 2010) that incorporate rigorous language demands across the content areas, all teachers will need to serve as role models. Kinsella suggests a schoolwide academic register campaign in which all teachers use an academic register consistently. She states, "Throughout the school day, students will rely on each and every teacher to adeptly articulate, demonstrate, and coach the foundational language and literacy skills of their discipline."

In order to create a schoolwide culture of elevated language, we must ensure that students have consistent exposure to academic language. Administrators can support this goal by establishing practices that enable students to access academic vocabulary across content areas with multiple exposures. In this chapter, we will look at three principals who led urban elementary schools in initiating a schoolwide campaign around academic vocabulary. We will also take a look at a small band of teachers who led a grassroots campaign of using academic vocabulary throughout their school.

Voices From the Field . . .

Rachel Esh: Principal of an Urban Elementary School

One such administrator is elementary school principal Rachel Esh, who implemented the principle of substitutionary language over the course of an entire school year through ongoing professional development for her staff. Rachel understood the value of teacher modeling of academic language as well as elevated language in general. As a result, she implemented a three-part series of professional development to build a schoolwide culture. The chart below highlights the focus of each session.

The authors had an opportunity to catch up with Rachel after the professional-development series. During their conversation, she reflected on the importance of the trainings in helping her staff understand the initiative and the role of collaboration in the process.

"How we speak is how we write."

As the principal of an elementary school with young learners, Rachel understands the impact of her students' listening and speaking skills on their literacy development. She explained that oftentimes, for our budding learners,

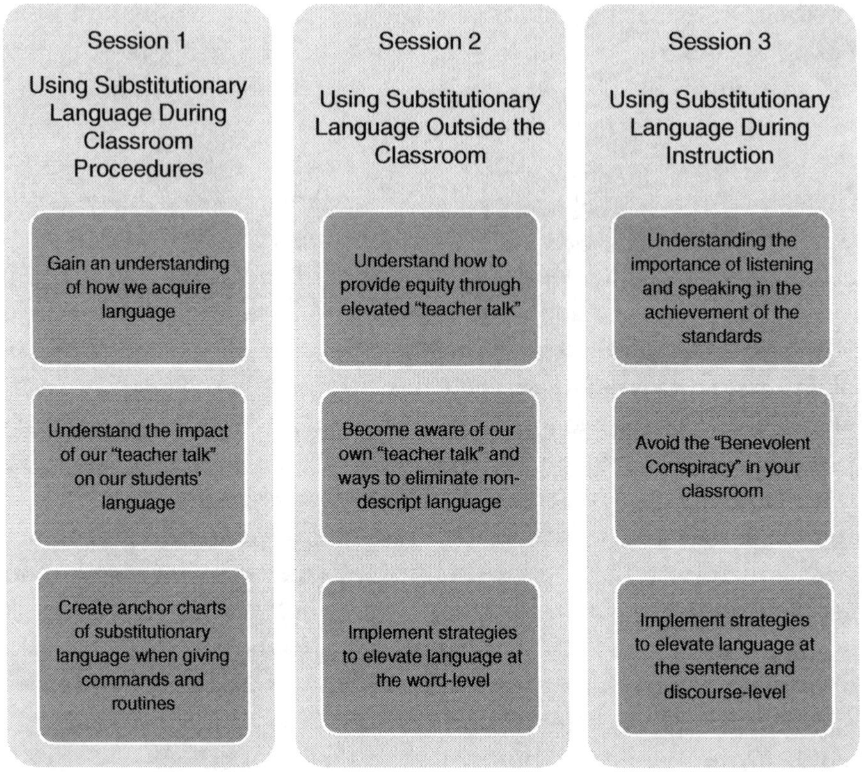

Figure 5.1 Substitutionary Language PD Highlights

"How they speak is how they write" (R. Esh, personal communication, May 4, 2022). To that end, she wholeheartedly supported the "Teacher Talk" trainings that promoted the principle of substitutionary speech. Rachel knew that if her students were exposed to elevated language on a consistent basis, across content areas, throughout the school day, it would eventually yield a positive return in their speaking as well as in their writing.

"If we're uncomfortable, we're learning."

Rachel explained how the professional-development sessions raised teachers' awareness of their own metacognition. She further explained the importance of open and honest communication in the process as her staff reflected on their own language choices throughout the school day. She realized her staff needed to make a conscious effort toward the consistent use of elevated language. Rachel recognized it was a challenging growth process but acknowledged, "If we're uncomfortable, we're learning" (R. Esh, personal communication, May 4, 2022).

"It comes down to collaboration."

Being intentional is key, according to Rachel. She has seen firsthand the impact of providing time for staff to collaborate. Highlighted among her observations was the following evidence:

- Grade-level teams created T-Charts of common language spoken across classrooms that could be replaced with more sophisticated words and phrases
- Teachers incorporated more precise language in question stems. Instead of, "Does anyone have any ideas to share?" teachers asked, "Does anyone have the evidence to support your opinion?"
- Teachers infused elevated language in content-area lessons, such as "answer" being replaced with "solution."

Rachel stated that she has seen an intentionality among her staff in using elevated language, an intentionality that has been fostered through collaboration. She emphasized, "It comes down to collaboration" (R. Esh, personal communication, May 4, 2022).

Wanda Ramirez-Suarez: School Leadership Coach

Wanda Ramirez-Suarez, a former elementary school principal who is currently serving as a school leadership coach, implemented a campaign to foster academic language in her school. Wanda stated, "We need to expose students to academic vocabulary because that is what gives them access to

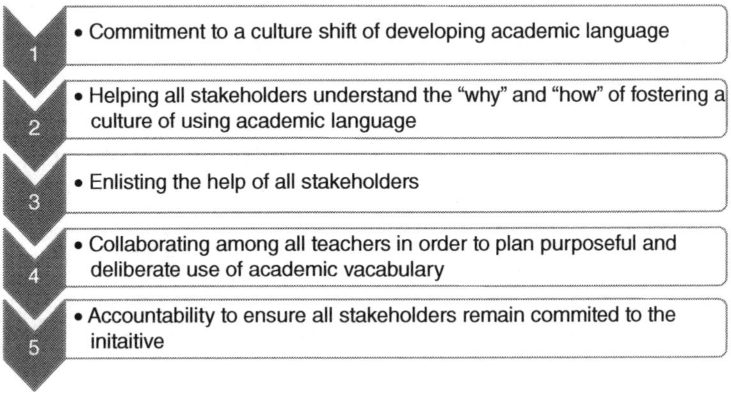

Figure 5.2 Key Elements in Establishing a School Wide Culture

opportunity. The opportunity to access academic texts and assessments as a result of educators explicitly teaching to the individual language needs of each child to ensure success. That's equity" (W. Ramirez-Suarez, personal communication, January 17, 2022). Wanda explained that there are several key elements in establishing a schoolwide culture of using rich academic vocabulary throughout the school building. These elements can be seen in the following table.

Creating a schoolwide culture of using elevated and academic language requires a commitment to shifting the culture in a school. It involves change, changes in the way we think and do. Wanda emphasized, "It's not a once and done, it's a culture-shift. This is how we are going to do business" (W. Ramirez-Suarez, personal communication, January 17, 2022). It is absolutely vital for school leaders to be committed to the culture-shift because it will take time and effort to equip teachers and staff and to get everyone moving in the same direction.

This leads to Wanda's next point: teachers and staff need to have buy-in when creating a culture in which everyone models the use of elevated and academic language. In order for all teachers to deeply understand the "why" and "how" of modeling this type of language, ongoing and sustained professional development needs to take place. Wanda equipped teachers throughout the year, over multiple years, through a variety of professional learning sessions, including: grade-level team meetings, after-school trainings, and schoolwide job embedded sessions, as well as targeted planning conversations and learning sessions with the English language development team. During these varied opportunities, staff gained knowledge on the importance of bolstering students' vocabularies and were equipped with strategies and routines for growing their academic vocabulary and precise language. They were given time to reflect on the concepts and create materials. In this way, all teachers and staff understood not only the "why" of using academic language but also how it would be accomplished.

To fully equip teachers and staff with the knowledge and strategies they would need to effectively model for students, Wanda enlisted the help of many stakeholders. Some of these stakeholders included teachers, building coaches, and districtwide specialty coaches, such as English language development coaches and literacy specialists. By enlisting the help of many stakeholders, Wanda was able to provide the ongoing and sustained professional development that is required to create a schoolwide culture.

The impact of these trainings was multiplied as teachers in Wanda's building were given time to collaborate with one another in order to provide interdisciplinary connections for students. She cited an example of collaboration in which a teacher explained that she would be teaching the concept of "perimeter." The physical education teacher was able to reinforce this concept by changing the command, "Run around the gymnasium" to "Run around the perimeter of the gymnasium." A simple change yielded big gains for these students, who were exposed to multiple repetitions of the word in a different context, all while physically experiencing the concept. Through collaboration, teachers were able to make explicit connections for students. Wanda emphasized that these connections would not happen without time given for the adults to plan and prepare.

Finally, Wanda cited accountability as a key factor in fostering a schoolwide culture. She regularly conducted informal observations and walkthroughs to support the schoolwide expectation that modeling high-level academic language and making connections for students is an expectation. The adage "we inspect what we expect" became the mantra by which Wanda and her teachers operated. Wanda suggested that accountability is often the missing link in efforts to create a schoolwide culture.

Many times, we associate the word "accountability" with negative connotations, catching someone not doing what they are supposed to be doing. While Wanda used observations and walkthroughs to identify teachers who were struggling to incorporate and model elevated language and provide support, she also used them to identify and highlight teachers who were incorporating strategies and seized the opportunity to take pictures and share strategies with the staff and all community stakeholders, often through the use of social media. The benefits of sharing these examples were twofold: they disseminated the knowledge and strategies across the school community and recognized the teachers as the true leaders in the initiative.

Camille Hopkins: Director of Schools in an Urban District

Camille Hopkins, former elementary school principal and current director of schools of an urban district, believes in the importance of equitable outcomes. As a master of creating a schoolwide culture, Camille stresses the importance of determining the what and the why of a school's professional-development focus. Camille emphasizes, "Everyone needs to be on the same page. Nothing can be done in isolation. This is a collective effort across the school. Collective ownership in which everyone has a voice" (C. Hopkins, personal communication, February 17, 2022).

In an interview with Camille in which she shared her action steps for creating a schoolwide culture, it became apparent that timely, detailed planning is instrumental in effectively implementing initiatives. The chart that follows details a year-long timeline of actionable items and the stakeholders involved in carrying out each item that was developed by Camille.

Before the School Year

Camille and her team started their planning in the summer. The entire team's mission and vision for the summer planning involved discovering students' strengths and areas of growth in order to build individual pathways for student success through an equity lens. Supporting the growth of students' language is one way to provide that equity.

Beginning of the School Year

Camille emphasized the importance of professional development at the beginning of every year in order to revisit the vision and mission of the district and school and to reset the goals, or focus areas, for the coming year. She also provided time during initial professional-development days for staff to discuss and collaborate around the goals. Through discussions and activities, the staff was able to assess their teaching practice in terms of bolstering students' language. Camille adds, "It is important to collect data to inform decisions when implementing a schoolwide initiative" (C. Hopkins, personal communication, February 17, 2022). The authors provide a self-assessment tool at the end of the chapter to be used individually by teachers, in groups as discussion questions, or by coaches and administrators during learning walks.

Throughout the Year

Throughout the year, teachers participated in and facilitated ongoing professional development in which the team shared and modeled their learning of best practices and strategies. Learning walks were an integral part in measuring the effectiveness of the professional-development learning and implementation of strategies.

Camille stated,

> As Dr. Rowe and I conducted learning walks over the years with language as a focus, we were able to identify specific learning behaviors that teachers had adopted from the professional learning. We observed teachers using the same effective strategies in their instructional delivery across grade levels, thus demonstrating all parties taking ownership of the schoolwide culture.

Camille emphasizes, as did Wanda Ramirez-Suarez, the importance of these learning walks as a means of "inspecting what you expect" (C. Hopkins, personal communication, February 17, 2022).

Timeline for Creating a School Wide Culture

Time Frame	Actionable Item	Stakeholder/s
Before the school year starts	• Analyze relevant data • Determine focus area needs: By looking at the data, can you determine the need to focus on language? • Gather stakeholders together to define the "What" and the "Why" • Map out professional development for the year • Create a tool in which to measure the use of substitutionary language in all areas of the school (see the example that follows) • Display anchor charts throughout the school as a reminder to use substitutionary language	All Staff Administration
Beginning of the Year	• Layout specific foci for all stakeholders • Collect baseline data from staff (see School Assessment Tool)	Administration
Throughout the Year	• Conduct classroom walkthroughs and collect data • Conduct informal and formal observations • Model substitutionary language throughout the school • Administer online self-assessment tool to staff to measure substitutionary language • Provide opportunities for collaboration among all staff members across grade levels and subject areas • Provide coaching by trained staff to assist in implementing substitutionary language	Administration All Staff

Camille concluded, "The success of the plan was the strong commitment of the English language development team, the special education team, and the instructional coach, who continue to be strong advocates and collaborators when it comes to looking for root causes of student success" (C. Hopkins, personal communication, February 17, 2022).

A Grassroots Movement . . . Jeanne Oakes and Yara Graupera, Teachers in an Urban District

While leading initiatives from the top down is likely the most common way of implementing initiatives, it's not the only way. ESL teachers Jeanne Oakes and Yara Graupera know the importance of speaking in an academic register with their English learners who are tasked with achieving the rigorous Common Core Standards and learning English at the same time. To that end, they embarked on a grassroots campaign of enlisting the teachers in their building to join their efforts.

In a short amount of time, Jeanne and Yara were able to enlist their colleagues teacher by teacher. Yara stated, "I think grassroots is probably the most impacting, because once it comes from leadership, it takes on a whole different feel" (Y. Graupera, personal communication, May 4, 2022).

Jeanne agreed, adding, "Top down versus bottom up, although they both have value, meeting in the middle can make a big impact" (J. Oakes, personal communication, May 4, 2022).

"It's a shift, a mind shift. It's not an extra thing that teachers have to prepare. It's not an extra thing, and that's part of the buy-in," Yara stated (Y. Graupera, personal communication, May 4, 2022).

To raise awareness among teachers, Jeanne and Yara created posters of elevated language that can be used when giving directions and hung them around the school as a reminder to teachers and students alike that there are alternative ways of saying common vocabulary words. Yara noted, "The teachers are thinking about it, and that's the first step" (Y. Graupera, personal communication, May 4, 2022).

Jeanne and Yara took their students on a field trip to take notice of the posters hanging around the school and to enlist their help.

Students and teachers quickly began using the words. Yara stated, "I can't tell you how many times I have heard teachers say 'Proceed in line,' or the students say, 'I'm proceeding to the bathroom' or 'Can I dispense the books?'" She added, "The kids are excited to sound smart" (Y. Graupera, personal communication, May 4, 2022).

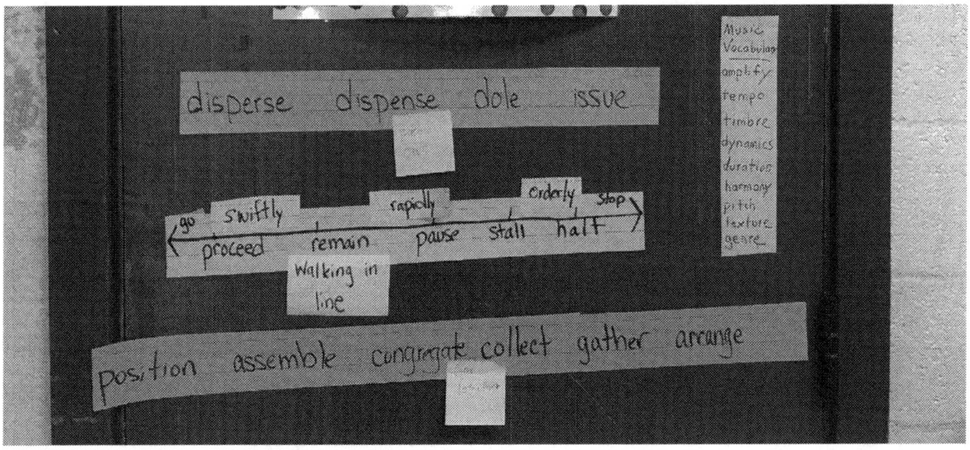

Figure 5.3 Example of School Wide Poster on Door

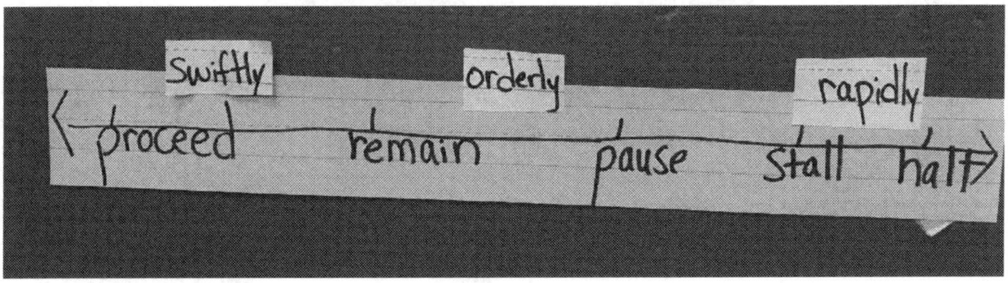

Figure 5.4 Example of School Wide Poster in Cafeteria

Both Jeanne and Yara agreed that teachers need to begin by having a conversation about academic register, explaining what it is. Yara explained that while she rarely uses Tier 2 and Tier 3 academic vocabulary at home in social conversations, her students need to be exposed to it because it is the language they will encounter in the various content areas. "It's taking the implicit and making it explicit," Yara explained (Y. Graupera, personal communication, May 4, 2022).

Students are beginning to take initiative on using sophisticated language and contributing to a culture within the school in which everyone uses an academic register. One student suggested to Ms. Graupera, "I have a fancier word for water. We could say, 'Let's hydrate' instead of 'Can I go get a drink?' " That in turn led to a discussion about "dehydrate." In the end, it was decided to make signs above the drinking fountains that say, "Don't forget to hydrate!" Students are becoming more conscious about their word choices (Y. Graupera, personal communication, May 4, 2022).

The teachers noted that the morning announcements have taken on a new tenor as well. Tier 1 vocabulary words have been replaced with Tier 2 vocabulary words. An example is, "Initiate your work of the day" and "Initiate the Pledge of Allegiance." The classroom teacher then picked up on it, using it immediately. "It's spreading. There's an interest there among teachers and a consciousness about words among students," Yara stated (Y. Graupera, personal communication, May 4, 2022).

To include the counselor and emotional support teachers, Jeanne and Yara provided these teachers with relationship words and mindset words. Examples of these words include:

Positive Relationship Words	Mindset Words
• Gracious • Impartial • Sincere • Polite • Considerate • Genuine	• Accomplish • Logical • Ambitious • Curious • Creative • Active

Cognates of the words above were provided for English learners.

Getting Started—Collecting Baseline Data

Some administrators might wonder where to get started. It is helpful for administrators to collect baseline data in order to gauge whether staff are using elevated language across content areas throughout the school day. Following is a tool to do just that. The tool is based on our strategies. Administrators can use this tool during informal observations, or they may reflect on walk-throughs that they have conducted thus far in the year. The purpose of this tool is to give administrators and schools a general overview, or finger on the pulse, of the use of elevated language in their school. Please keep in mind, this should not be a "gotcha" for teachers, nor should teachers be singled out.

School Self-Assessment Tool

Criteria/Tennant Point Value	Always 3	Occasionally 2	Seldom 1	Never 0	Not Sure 0
Inside the Classroom (Teacher specific)					
Teachers use a formal register throughout the school day devoid of informal contractions (words such as cuz, gonna, OK, etc.).					
Teachers use specific language as opposed to vague language (stuff and things).					
Teachers use substitutionary language while giving directions. For example, "Proceed to the front of the room" as opposed to "Come to the front of the room."					
Teachers substitute common words with words with more nuanced meaning. For example, "old" becomes "ancient"; "happy" becomes "elated."					
Teachers use content specific vocabulary throughout the school day without confining its use to the social studies, science, and mathematics classrooms.					
Teachers teach multiple meaning words.					
Teachers model signal words (transition words) in spoken discourse.					
Teachers use figurative language such as similes, metaphors, and idioms throughout the day.					

Teachers use the concept of word families to expand students' vocabularies.					
Teachers seize those teachable moments to speak in discourse.					
Teachers address the standards orally when having conversations with students.					
Teachers relate character traits and themes to their students' lives, for example, relating the theme of perseverance and the character trait of tenacity to a student's resolve to not give up.					
Outside the Classroom					
Evidence exists of staff using elevated vocabulary in common areas of the school such as the cafeteria and the playground.					

Reflection Questions

1. What did you notice?

   ____

   ____

2. Do the results surprise you?

   ____

   ____

3. What are your strongest areas?

   ____

   ____

4. What are your weakest areas?

   ____

   ____

Scoring Guidelines

31–39 Strong evidence of a schoolwide culture of elevated language
21–30 Evidence of elevated language among groups of teachers
11–20 Isolated attempts of elevated language in the school
0–10 Little or no evidence of elevated language in the school

Conclusion

Think of the impact! The power of all teachers across grade levels and specialists buying into the concept of using elevated language all day, every day with their students. The students would hear words multiple times a day, in a variety of contexts, from a variety of staff members. They would value these words because their teachers were using them. Eventually, these words would become part of their vocabularies without being explicitly taught.

References

Common Core State Standards. (2010). *Applications of Common Core State Standards for English language arts & literacy in history/social studies, science, and technical subjects*. www.corestandards.org

Kinsella, K. (2018). Cutting to the common core: Disrupting discourse. *Language Magazine*, January 30, 2018.

Shanahan, T. (2005). *The national reading panel report. Practical advice for teachers.* Learning Point Associates/North Central Regional Educational Laboratory (NCREL).

6

Engaging Caregivers to Use Elevated Language

I have found that once an effort is being made to elevate language spoken to children, it provides endless benefits in their work with reading, writing and speaking vocabulary. Having been a teacher at the elementary level for 34 years, I enforce and strongly encourage parents, caregivers and teaching professionals to embrace the use of elevated language in everyday conversations.

~Vicki Legath, Veteran Teacher and Grandmother
(V. Legath, personal communication, January 29, 2022)

Introduction

"Parents are their children's first and most influential teachers. What parents do to help their children learn is more important to academic success than how well-off the family is" (U.S. Department of Education, 1986). This impact also affects their children's language development.

Pediatricians created the term "language nutrition" to emphasize to caregivers that it is vital for children to be exposed to rich language through social interactions for the well-being of their development and health. According to Kapengut and Noble (2020), children benefit when their caregivers use frequent, varied, and complex speech. The researchers further stated, "differences in the home language environment lead to early differences in language and reading-related skills, which in turn serve as precursors of later academic achievement" (p. 74).

In Chapter 3 we discussed the common order in which children acquire the four language skills: listening, speaking, reading, and writing. While there

DOI: 10.4324/9781003295716-7

are anomalies to this order, it is the general order in which children learn language. The Common Core State Standards (2010) document emphasized, "For children in preschool and the early grades, receptive and expressive abilities do not develop simultaneously or at the same pace; receptive language generally precedes expressive language. Children need to be able to understand words before they can produce and use them." The research is replete with findings on the importance of creating a language-rich environment for children from the earliest of ages and beyond. The authors recognize the important role of caregivers in the development of a child's robust vocabulary.

This chapter will focus on strategies for caregivers to use in maximizing their roles in developing and bolstering language with their children. We will also offer tips for parents when implementing the strategies and discuss the school's role in supporting caregivers when implementing the strategies.

Strategies for Caregivers to Use With Their Children

The strategies included are focused on common everyday occurrences. Genishi (1988) suggests that exposing children to experiences is vital and that the experiences are as important as the words we use to make sense of those experiences. Genishi goes on to say, "words are learned, not taught, in contexts and activities that teachers have arranged and sustained often through talk" (p. 23). Carmen recalls her four-year-old granddaughter, Liv, saying, "Grammie, we can use the playground if school isn't in session." How had Liv known to use the expression "in session"? She had acquired it through repeated modeling by her parents and older sisters.

Talking to your child about even the smallest details of life not only assures your child of your attention to them but also helps them make sense of their worlds and words. Explaining the colors and purpose of a traffic signal as you are walking on the sidewalk or driving down the street is one opportunity to develop language. For example, you might say, "The red light means stop, the green light means go, and the yellow light means slow down, be cautious, or be careful, a red light is coming, get ready, or prepare, to stop." When this explanation is supported with gestures, voice intonation, and facial expressions, we can aid our children's understanding of new vocabulary connected to experiences right in the moment. In-the-moment vocabulary instruction can occur with preschool-aged children, as well as elementary-aged, by seizing routine and commonplace occurrences to expose them to new vocabulary. These everyday events provide endless opportunities to bolster our children's vocabularies. The chart that follows takes our traffic light example and shows the potential of expanding children's vocabularies during one small event in the day.

Categories	Vocabulary Words	Sentence With Simple Language	Sentence With Substitutionary Language
Verbs	Red light yellow light green light	The red light means stop. The yellow light means slow down and stop. The green light means go.	The red light signals stop. The yellow light signals slow down and stop. The green light signals go.
Commands/ Directives	Stop. Get ready. Go.	Stop at the red light. Get ready to stop. Go at the green light.	Come to a halt at the red light. Prepare to stop. Proceed at the green light.
Nouns	Traffic light/ signal light Intersection	The traffic light is located in the street.	The signal light is located in the intersection.
Units of Time	Seconds, minutes	We slow down when the light turns red. The light stays green.	We have seconds to slow down when the light turns red. The light remains red for a minute or two.

Genishi (1988) proposed that children's language learning "proceeds from action or experience to concept to words, and not from word to concept to experience" (p. 18). Understanding this progression can help us capitalize on the everyday experiences that are part of our children's worlds and help them make sense of these experiences, starting with simple language and gradually substituting in more sophisticated and precise vocabulary. So what types of experiences can parents seize as teaching moments? All experiences, from the commonplace daily routines to the unexpected hectic and chaotic occurrences that are part of life, can serve up opportunities to model elevated language.

After being introduced to the concept of using elevated language by the authors of this book, Vicki Legath began deliberately using it expressively with her four-year-old granddaughter. She found that before long, it was gradually being used naturally and purposefully in their everyday conversations. Her granddaughter became curious and inquisitive about the meaning of words.

She asked, "What does that mean?" each time Legath used a new word in context. Legath began looking at everyday life occurrences as opportunities to model elevated language. For example, as they pass an airport near their home each week, her granddaughter now asks, "I wonder if we will see any arrivals or departures today?" In the past, she would ask if any planes were coming or leaving. Legath witnessed the fruits of her labor after attending a local town parade and collecting candy that was being thrown from parade floats. Her granddaughter exclaimed as they were walking back to the car, "We have an abundance of candy." Legath is not the only one who has noticed her granddaughter's robust vocabulary. In a recent conversation with the authors, Legath shared that her granddaughter's teacher has also noticed her vocabulary.

Reflection Questions

1. Brainstorm a list of common everyday occurrences or events in your life, for example: getting dressed in the morning, picking up toys, or packing a backpack.

   ____

   ____

   ____

2. Pick one of the events that you brainstormed above and jot it down in column 1. List the language typically associated with those occurrences in column 2. In column 3, consider how you might substitute higher-level vocabulary instead of the commonplace words.

Column 1	Column 2	Column 3
Common Event	**Language: What are common words you use in each scenario?** Write the words in complete sentences. Underline a common word in each sentence that could be replaced by more sophisticated language.	**Rewrite the sentence with the common word replaced with the more sophisticated word.**
Ex. Brushing teeth	Brush your **top** and **bottom** teeth.	Brush your **upper** and **lower** teeth.
1.		
2.		
3.		

We can model language for children in a variety of ways and events, including preparing meals, mealtime, emotions, bedtime routines, singing, reciting rhymes, taking walks, storytelling, games, getting ready for school, and math moments, just to mention a few examples. Every event in the home and excursions outside of the home with family members and caregivers provides opportunities to model elevated language to children. Predicting the language used in each scenario allows the caregiver an opportunity to adjust his or her speech in a planned manner. In addition to seizing the everyday moments of life to expose children to elevated language, parents can also take time for creating their own stories to share with their children, singing songs and chants, and routinely reciting poetry.

Storytelling

Introduction

"Storytelling is universal and is as ancient as humankind. Before there was writing, there was storytelling. It occurs in every culture and from every age. It exists (and existed) to entertain, to inform, and to promulgate cultural traditions and values" (National Geographic, 2020). Children learn so much through storytelling. They learn about themselves, others, and the world around them. Carmen recounts her husband, Rick's, storytelling with their eight children. "While all these stories opened up our children to new worlds and fostered their imagination, it also helped impart our values and beliefs," states Carmen. "From a language perspective, each story introduced our children to new vocabulary words," she added.

Rationale

Watson (1987) found that young elementary children retained the meaning of new words when they were learned in the context of stories. The act of storytelling with family members helps to develop intellectual skills such as critical thinking, perspective-taking, and metacognition, all skills that are valued in mainstream education (Ochs et al., 1992). Genishi (1988) suggested that language-rich environments have a replay quality about them in which

> A word may be repeated 20 times or more, not in the senseless context of an isolated sentence, but in a range of contexts: a poem, a child-created song or drama, a caption for a drawing, a chant, a story that children beg to hear again, a game that a child plays and replays with friends, or a conversation with children or the teacher.
>
> (p. 22)

In addition to sharpening listening skills and fostering children's imagination, storytelling helps with the sequencing of events and taking a third-person perspective. Let's take a look at how one of these stories might take shape.

Description

The author, Carmen, and her husband, Rick Rowe, raised their eight children beside a field full of rabbits, so it made perfect sense to Rick that these small creatures should become the main characters in his nightly bedtime tales to their children. These tales often included a retelling of the day's adventures including successes, mishaps, and lessons learned. Since the stories were based on their familiar, lived experiences from the day just spent, the Rowe children were held captive with these recollections in story form. While the tales were laden with interesting details, most noteworthy was the rich vocabulary and suspense virtues that filled each story from start to finish.

An excerpt of one of Rick's stories follows:

> *Once upon a time, there were two rabbit boys, Hoppy and Happy. They had three sisters and a mom and dad. How many lived in the rabbit hole? Yes! Seven rabbits lived together in their home! Now the rabbit hole was <u>located</u> in a very cozy <u>location</u> at the edge of a forest, and the rabbit boys loved where they lived! One day, they grew enough to <u>venture</u> outside, so Papa Rabbit <u>called a meeting</u> at the kitchen table. "Hop and Hap," Papa said, for those were their nicknames, "you have now grown <u>sufficiently</u> to leave our home to <u>venture</u> outside. But I have some rules you must obey in order to keep you safe. Always stay together and look out for one another. Never <u>stray</u> so far that you get lost. <u>Finally</u>, and <u>most importantly</u>, the number one rule is to never, ever leave the forest to play in the farmer's field that is <u>located</u> beside it! Without the cover of the trees, hawks might see you and <u>descend upon</u> you and carry you away. And even <u>more probable</u> than that is the <u>possibility</u> that the farmer will catch you both. He would like nothing more than to make a nice rabbit stew out of you!*

Not long ago, Rick and Carmen had the pleasure of keeping their grandsons, Jack and Tommy, overnight. It should be noted that their daughter, Abby, has continued the story-telling tradition with her boys. "As we tucked the boys in one evening, Tommy, our three-year-old grandson, asked if he could tell a rabbit story," recalls Carmen. He did. Starting with, "Once there were . . ." Although the beginning, middle, and end were a little difficult to follow at times, the story was replete with transition words, such as "so" and "then," to connect events.

Ideas in Practice

Using the literary device for summarizing stories known as "Somebody wanted . . . but . . . so . . . then . . ." we'll take you through an exercise of creating an engaging story with characters that will appeal to your children and will have them coming back for more tales. While you'll need to add rich details to your story to captivate your children's interest, the storytelling generator will help you clarify the basic premise, or plot, of your story. The story chart shows how Rick's rabbit story could be developed.

Storytelling Generator

Somebody wanted	Hoppy and Happy want to go into the farmer's field to play
But	their father told them to stay together and never stray far away
So	they disobeyed their father and hopped into the farmer's open field
Then	two hawks swooped down and carried them away

Most stories follow this repeating pattern of events: "Somebody wanted . . . but . . . so . . . then . . ." All good stories, at their core, have characters who want something that they can't have. That is the conflict, the suspense. Then it's up to you to decide just how the story will resolve. Maybe your character or characters will get what they want, or maybe they won't get what they want but will learn the value of patience.

Put It Into Practice

Now it's your turn to give storytelling a try! Use the story generator that follows or create a story on your own to start a tradition of storytelling in your home.

Storytelling Generator

Somebody wanted	
But	
So	
Then	

Memorized Songs, Chants, and Poetry

Most songs, chants, and poetry all have a rhythm, or cadence, that makes them pleasurable to recite. Children love familiarity, and songs, chants, and poetry provide just that. When children are repeatedly exposed to these, it gives them the opportunity to practice pronunciation and fluency and to learn many new words.

Songs and Chants

Introduction

Carmen's husband Rick, a musician by trade, recalls the story of when he was in kindergarten and was asked by his teacher to recite the letters of the alphabet. While he was unable to recite the alphabet by just speaking it, when invited to sing it, he was able to do so, letter perfect, all to the tune of the alphabet song. Songs are a great vehicle through which to teach language. Likewise, chants have been used by teachers and parents of elementary-aged students to teach not only new routines but also new vocabulary. Sarah Rowe, the author's daughter and a teacher, underscores the importance of music in learning, "When I taught preschool, we had a song to teach letter sounds. Ninety percent of our students knew all their sounds before they knew their letters. Rote memory and music go hand in hand" (S. Rowe, personal communication, May 15, 2022).

Chants are another way to teach language to young children in a fun manner, as these typically are a short sentence or two and fun to recite in a singsong way.

Description

Finding sources of children's music and chants is not difficult. A search on the internet yields scores of sources. While music videos are plentiful, there's no substitute for parents stopping their daily duties, getting down on their children's level, and singing songs with them. Find songs and start singing with your children, and do it regularly! No age is too early.

Chants are sentences that are spoken or shouted, repeatedly, in a singsong way. These can include prayers or ditties created for specific purposes.

Rationale

The youngest of children can build their receptive and productive vocabularies through listening to and singing along with music. Carmen's daughter-in-law, Alaina, affirmed the importance of music for their son, Canaan. She stated, "Canaan has certainly learned words through singing and listening to music. Even at 21 months, he can recognize these words in conversation that trace back to a melody he has heard over and over again." Alaina then went on to cite just a few of the words he has learned and now uses in his own speech: rain, happy, bumblebee, joy, muffin, bath, water, bus, now, me, I, and heart.

The author's daughter-in-law, Lauren, affirmed the impact music has had on their daughter Kate's, language. The nursery song "One Little Finger" was incredibly helpful in teaching Kate the concept of "one," different body parts, different actions like tapping, and some directions.

Carmen's daughter-in-law, Tori, has made a ritual of singing to her children, Grace and Hudson. Songs such as "You Are My Sunshine" and "I Love You a Bushel and a Peck" create an affectionate moment for them as well as expose them to figurative language such as "You make me happy when skies are gray" and the quantities "a bushel" and "a peck."

Ideas in Practice

Chants are purposeful and fun. In our home, they served as a trigger for routines: the routine to get ready for school or the routine to settle down for bedtime. Carmen recalls, "In our home, we created many chants, such as:

- Getting ready for school: 'Don't forget your hair, teeth, hands, and face!'
- At bedtime: 'God bless you from the top of your head to the tips of your toes and even your cute little nose.' "

Chants can provide security for our children, a familiarity that denotes a common routine. Take time to start family traditions that include these short quips.

Songs include all types of music written for a variety of purposes, seasons, and genres. Listening to songs repeatedly gives multiple exposures to not only the message but also language. It's never too early to begin exposing children to music. A good place to start is common nursery rhymes such as: "The Itsy-Bitsy Spider" and "The Wheels on the Bus." While these are two common examples in English, nursery rhymes exist in any culture. Commit to singing songs in your home. The QR code that follows provides the reader with an alphabetically arranged list of nursery rhymes as well as songs, lullabies, and chants for younger children. In addition to the title of each rhyme, the site includes a short description of each.

Nursery Rhyme List

Reflection Question

1. Take some time to research songs. Jot down the names of those you believe your children might enjoy during the following times of the year. Some tune titles are already filled in for you.

Playlist for the ______________________ Family	
Topic	Songs
Seasons: winter, spring, summer, fall	Winter: "Sleigh Ride"
Holidays	Fourth of July: "The Star-Spangled Banner"
Family, Mother's Day, Father's Day, Siblings' Day	Family: "We Are Family"
Motivational	"The Eye of the Tiger"
Vacations	"In the Good Old Summertime"
Friendship	"Lean on Me," "You've Got a Friend"

Now that you've created a playlist for your family, be intentional about carving time out of the day to listen to a song or two. "In our family with eight children, each day found us waiting or traveling, often by car, to and from events. These were prime times to listen to music and discuss the lyrics," Carmen recalls. She recounts the following example of driving in the car with her two daughters, listening to one of their favorite tunes, Dolly Parton's "Working Nine to Five." After singing through the tune together, her youngest daughter, Abby, asked, "What does 'nine to five' mean?" A quick discussion of common work hours ensued all because of the lyrics of a song.

Poetry

Introduction

Rhymes and poetry are great ways to teach precise and nuanced vocabulary to students through oral language. Carmen recollects several poems recited repeatedly as part of a tradition with their children. One of these poems was "Pussy Willow" by Aileen Fisher. Each year, when our pussy willow bush bloomed, we clipped several branches to bring indoors, and thus would began a season of not only enjoying these beautiful fuzzy-laden buds, but also the recitation of the "Pussy Willow" poem. The poem invites children to close their eyes and not peek as "spring" is rubbed across their cheek. Our toddlers and even older children, most likely too ashamed to admit it, would all close their eyes, sometimes reciting the poem, too, but always waiting with anticipation for the beautiful, familiar words in rhyming cadence while the soft pussy willows were rubbed across their cheeks. This is the power of poetry. In addition to fostering a love for poetry, our children were exposed to words such as "smooth," "sleek," and "satin."

Description

This strategy requires that you specifically choose poems suited to your child's age and interests to read aloud on a regular basis. While introducing new poems creates interest in the genre, reading the same ones repeatedly allows children to memorize the poem and acquire new vocabulary and sentence structures.

Rationale

Including poetry as part of your interactions with the children in your home has many benefits. Giannikas (2017) notes that poetry helps teach children new vocabulary as well as language structures that might be less used in social speech. Kane (1998) encourages the use of poetry as a means of exposing children to and teaching them about rhyme, rhythm, repetition, symbolism and content (p. 435). Phonological awareness is an awareness of the sounds spoken in any given language. Exposing young children to poetry helps them develop the ability to identify words that rhyme, an essential phonological prereading skill.

Ideas in Action

The power of poetry is that with repeated readings, children will come to memorize each verse, and with it new vocabulary, rhyming words, figurative language, and a different structure of language. For preschoolers and early elementary students, nursery rhymes are a great place to start. If you know your child has particular interests, find a poem on the topic to ensure engagement.

Reflection Question

2. Take some time to research poetry written by some famous children's writers: Walter de la Mare, A.A. Milne, Valerie Bloom, Robert Louis Stevenson, Roald Dahl, Dr. Seuss, Shel Silverstein, and Carmen's personal favorite, Robert Southey, who wrote "The Cataract of Lodore." You can search for poems online or at your local

library. Jot down the titles of some of the poems you enjoyed the most and believe your children would find interesting. Beside the title, write the authors who wrote them.

____

____

____

When reading the poem aloud, here are some tips to make the experience enjoyable and memorable.

- Recite the poem slowly but with lots of expression
- Emphasize the rhyming words
- Use hand motions as you say unfamiliar vocabulary words to add meaning
- Provide facial gestures to reinforce emotions represented in the poem or your own emotional response to the poem
- As you read the poem aloud, stop before the last word in each line and let your child say the word.

Making the reading and recitation of poetry a routine in your home will help build oral language skills and start a tradition that fosters a love for this genre of literature. Traditions and routines are powerful because they capitalize on creating a structure for repeatedly exposing our children to the sophisticated language of poetry. For example, perhaps every Friday evening, you set a few minutes aside for the reading of a poem. As your children become proficient readers, they, too, can join in the recitation. There are poems available on just about every topic imaginable, from brushing your teeth to playing with a pet.

Reflection Question

3. Choosing a regular time and place for reciting poems will help start a tradition in your family. How will you create a routine in which you read, teach, and recite poems in your home?

____

____

____

Tips for Parents When Implementing the Strategies

Speech modeled by caregivers to young children has the greatest impact when spoken directly to children. Weisleder and Fernald (2013) found, in children ages 19 to 24 months, that only speech spoken directly to the infant, and not speech in adult conversations overheard by the child, impacted their vocabulary learning at this age. The findings from this study are important to keep in mind with all children when implementing the strategies in this chapter.

There are many important ideas to keep in mind when speaking to your children during the implementation of any of the strategies in this chapter. First, giving your child your undivided attention shows that you are genuinely interested in them. Giving your full attention involves speaking directly to young children and is demonstrated by lowering one's body to be on eye level with the child and maintaining eye contact. You'll also want to move in close to the child. Practicing these skills as you speak to your child will also model good skills for your child when engaging in conversations with others.

The School's Role in Supporting Caregivers in Their Role of Bolstering Language

A synthesis of the research on the impact of caregivers on children's language yielded the following common supports related to strategies to bolster language: "coaching parents to talk more with their children, training parents to be responsive when their children initiate communication, and public awareness campaigns geared toward increasing parental knowledge of child development" (Kapengut & Noble, 2020, p. 81). The strategies presented in this chapter can all be coached by school personnel or caregivers. Raising caregivers' knowledge of how a child's language develops is important. In addition, helping them understand how they can help accelerate and bolster their children's language is key. Sax and Weston (2007) created the Language Development Milestones chart that can be used as a springboard for conversation.

Language Development Milestones (Sax & Weston, 2007)

Haase and Rowe emphasize that caregivers need to be trained in the strategies included in this chapter in order to equip them with the knowledge of implementing the strategies. The authors suggest that these strategies be shared with caregivers, one at a time, in workshops suited to the parents' schedules. The trainings should provide caregivers an opportunity to observe the strategies being modeled as well as an opportunity for support as they try them out on the spot. These trainings could be led by teachers, administrators, or parent leaders.

References

Common Core State Standards for English Language Arts. (2010). Appendix A.

Genishi, C. (1988). Children's language: Learning words from experience. *Young Children*, *44*(1), 16–23. www.jstor.org/stable/42728549

Giannikas, C. (2017). Poetry, please! *English Teaching Professional*, *110*, 27–28.

Kane, S. (1998). Teaching skills within meaningful contexts. *The Reading Teacher*, *51*(5), 434–436.

Kapengut, D., & Noble, K. G. (2020). Parental language and learning directed to the young child. *The Future of Children*, *30*(2), 71–92.

National Geographic. (2020). *Storytelling and other cultural traditions*. www.nationalgeographic.org/article/storytelling-and-cultural-traditions/

Ochs, E., Taylor, C., Rudolph, D., & Smith, R. (1992). Storytelling as theory-building activity. *Discourse Processes*, *15*, 37–72.

Sax, N., & Weston, E. (2007). *Language development milestones*. University of Alberta.

United States Department of Education. (1986). *What works: Research about teaching and learning*. Author.

Watson, R. (1987). Learning words from linguistic expressions: Definition and narrative. *Research in the Teaching of English*, *21*, 298–317.

Weisleder, A., & Fernald, A. (2013). Talking to children matters: Early language experience strengthens processing and builds vocabulary. *Psychological Science*, *24*, 2143–2152. https://doi.org/10.1177/0956797613488145

Index

Note: Page numbers in *italics* indicate a figure.